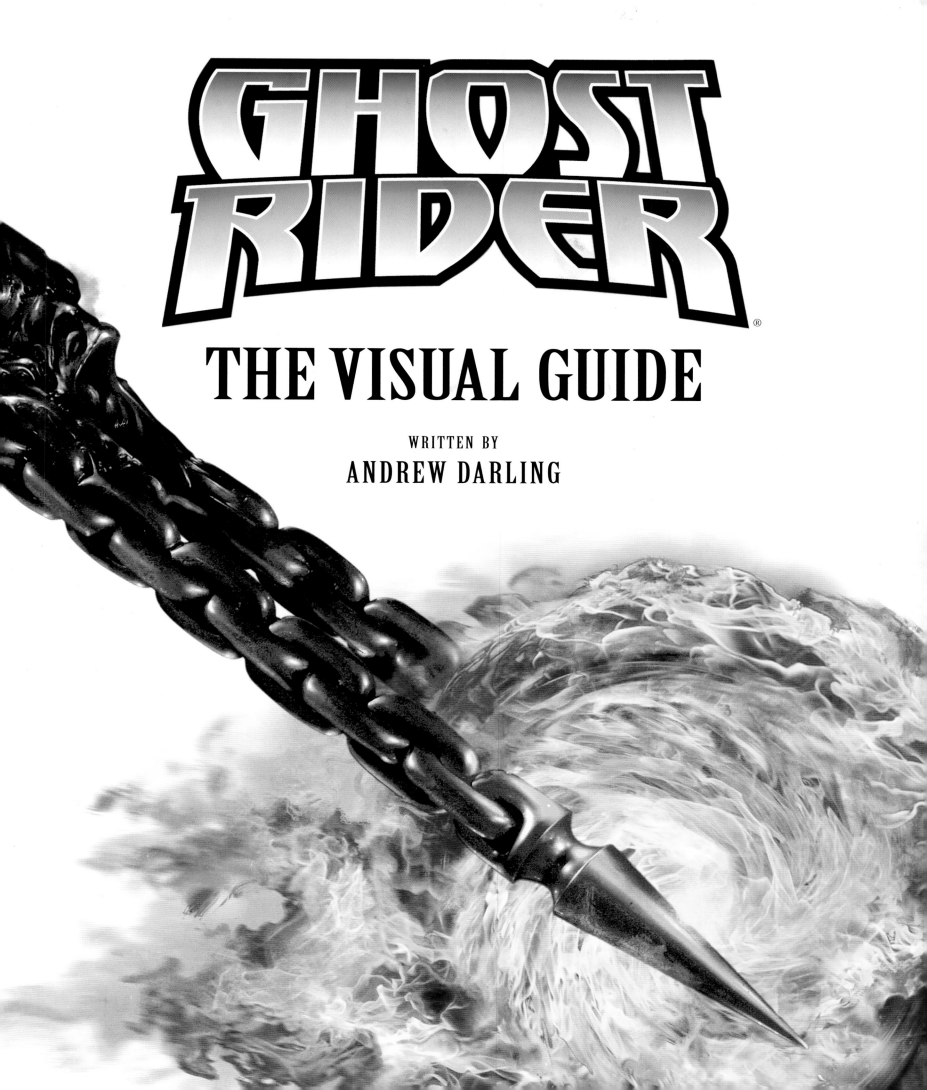

GHOST RIDER

THE VISUAL GUIDE

WRITTEN BY
ANDREW DARLING

CONTENTS

Foreword   6

CHAPTER 1: ORIGINS

Introduction   10
The Ghost Riders   12
Zarathos   14
Mephisto   16

CHAPTER 2: JOHNNY BLAZE

Introduction   20
Johnny Blaze   22
The Coming of the Ghost Rider   24
Crash Simpson and Roxanne Simpson   26
The Powers of Johnny Blaze   28
Johnny Blaze's Bike   30
Copperhead Canyon   32
The Champions   34
The Wilderness Years   36
The Orb and Water Wizard   38
Flagg Fargo and Azmodeus   40
Quentin Carnival   42
Centurious   44
A Town Called Holly   46

CHAPTER 3: DAN KETCH

Introduction   50
Dan Ketch   52
Noble Kale   54
A Noble Ghost Rider   56
Dan Ketch's Powers   58
Stacy Dolan   60
Francis Ketch and Captain Dolan   62
Allies   64
Ghost Rider meets Ghost Rider   66
Caretaker   68

Deathwatch   70
Blackout   72
Vengeance   74
Scarecrow and Zodiak   76
Lilith   78
Midnight Sons   80

CHAPTER 4: GHOST RIDER JOURNEYS ON

Introduction   84
John Blaze and the Quentin Carnival   86
Regent   88
Hellgate   90
Code:Blue and Jennifer Kale   92
Blackheart   94
A Ghost Rider No More?   96
Icebox Bob and Blaze's Children   98
Ghost Rider Returns   100
Road to Damnation   102
Ghost Rider 2099   104
Ghost Rider: The Movie   106
Allies and Enemies   108

THE COMICS

1970s   112
1970s and 1980s   114
1990s Part 1   116
1990s Part 2   118
1990s Part 3   120
1990s Part 4   122
2000s   124
Index   126
Acknowledgments   128

GHOST RIDER IN THE SKY

The Ghost Rider rode a long trail before he materialized in the pages of Marvel Comics in 1973—and he's ridden just as far since.

And it all began... with a song.

One of the hottest tunes on the radio in 1949 was "Riders in the Sky." Well, that was its official title, but I never heard anyone refer to it as anything but "Ghost Riders in the Sky," since that's the famous lyric. It was apparently written by a guy named Stan Jones, who in 1926 had, as an impressionable boy of 12, been told by an old hermit the story of phantom cowboys doomed to ride the sky forever in pursuit of the devil's cattle herd.

The song was recorded first by Roy Rogers (yep, the ol' King of the Cowboys himself) and the Sons of the Pioneers. The big hit version of '49 was by deep-voiced Vaughn Monroe. But for my money the one that wiped 'em all out was Frankie Laine's. Over the years it's been recorded by a lot of good singers, from Marty Robbins to Johnny Cash to Tom Jones to Burl Ives to, believe it or not, Peggy Lee. Walter Brennan talked his way through it once... and Spike Jones made glorious fun of it. Duane Eddy, R.E.M., and the Ventures all did instrumental versions. It's a great song... one of the best pop tunes ever, in many people's opinions. Including the opinion of this writer, who was eight going on nine when it came out.

So when, in 1950, I spotted a comic book titled *Ghost Rider*, I immediately picked it up and I loved it— and I never for a moment doubted where its name and inspiration came from. That first comic-book Ghost Rider I'd seen—there'd been another one, in the early 1940s, but it hadn't amounted to much—was the brainstorm of a small company called Magazine Enterprises (M.E.). This Ghost Rider was a secret-identity Western hero, garbed from head to foot—hat to boot—in white. And so was his horse! In this spectral guise, marshal Rex Fury terrified outlaws by pulling off stunts that seemed supernatural, but there was always a real-world gimmick behind them. *Ghost Rider* spirited along nicely until the Comics Code brought a halt to his nocturnal rides in 1954. Can't have ghosts—even make-believe ones—scaring the kiddies, can we?

Ghost Rider, however, had made a strong impression on someone at Marvel Comics. Although, as Stan Lee's associate editor in 1966, I first heard about Marvel's plans to launch the Western weirdo in its own lineup from The Man himself, I couldn't swear it wasn't publisher Martin Goodman who had that particular brainstorm. It was a natural. After all, Dick Ayers, the artist who'd drawn every single *Ghost Rider* story at M.E., was drawing for Marvel in the '60s. Dick has said that Stan complimented him on his work on the M.E. character when they first met in the early '50s. As soon as I learned there'd be a *Ghost Rider* mag at Marvel, I put in dibs on writing it. Stan agreed, but later changed his mind because he didn't want me "wasting my time" on a Western when I could be writing more Super Heroes. So the task went to my old friend Gary Friedrich, and I merely co-plotted the first issue with him. Marvel's first *Ghost Rider* appeared with a February 1967 cover date, and a powerful cover by Ayers. Because the original Ghost Rider was an "abandoned trademark," Marvel could make the character look exactly as he had in the '50s, but apparently we couldn't use the Rex Fury secret identity, so he became Carter Slade, a school teacher.

Unfortunately, Westerns weren't exactly the coming thing in the late '60s, and *Ghost Rider* was canceled after a mere seven bimonthly issues. Those stories would be reprinted over the years, with an occasional new one being done, though with the name of the cryptic cowboy changed to "Night Rider" or "Phantom Rider"—because of what happened in 1972.

And what happened then, once again, involved Gary Friedrich and myself.

I had inherited the scripting of Marvel's *Daredevil* from Stan Lee, and for that series had created a motorcycle-riding villain called the Sportsmaster. He wasn't much of a bad guy, if I do say so myself—and I do. Soon afterward, Gary, who was on staff as an assistant editor, took over *Daredevil* because I was busy with my duties as associate editor and with other scripting. Gary soon decided it was time for Ol' Hornhead to face a heller on wheels, but he didn't particularly care for the Sportsmaster, either. Instead, he came to me one day in the office and said he'd like to make up a new villain on a motorcycle—and call him the Ghost Rider!

I thought about it for a minute, and then responded, "I don't think we should do that."

Gary looked at me like I was crazy. Didn't I recognize a good idea when I heard one?

My next line was: "I think that's too good an idea to waste on a villain. We should make him a hero."

Gary smiled. Maybe I wasn't as loony as I looked.

Stan liked the idea so much, when we told him about it, that he immediately okayed the concept of starring this Ghost Rider in a mag all by himself. I've no memory of whether that had been in Gary's mind or in mine, or if we were just checking to make sure it was okay to make up a villainous Ghost Rider. At this point, I don't believe we had much of anything but the name and mode of transportation. Was he originally intended to be a guy just pretending to be a spirit, like the Western hero? Seems logical, since we weren't in the habit of pitting Daredevil against real ghosts.

At any rate, Ghost Rider metamorphosed almost at once into a truly supernatural Super Hero. After all, this was the era when, with the Comics Code having been forced to loosen up a bit, we were launching characters like Dracula, Werewolf by Night, Morbius the Living Vampire, Man-Thing, et al., in their own magazines... and this new Ghost Rider fitted right in with that bunch!

Far as I recall, Gary handled the story side of his brimstone-spouting brainchild pretty much by his lonesome. But Stan and I both knew the perfect artist for the title: Michael Ploog. Mike, who had come to Marvel from a job assisting the great Will Eisner, had a drawing style that would've been right at home on Eisner's earlier series, *The Spirit*—and it was perfect for this Ghost Rider, as well.

The only other thing I recall is the day the character was to be visually designed. That morning, Mike and I got to work—him drawing, me looking over his shoulder and kibitzing—I told him I wanted Ghost Rider to wear a full-length, black-leather, tight-fitting motorcycle suit. This was based on the black-leather jumpsuit Elvis Presley had worn in one famous segment of his 1968 "comeback special" on TV. Both Gary and I had been huge Elvis fans since the mid-'50s, and we had watched that special together at my apartment a few years earlier.

I told Mike I thought this Ghost Rider's head should be a skull. Mike started drawing away... and suddenly I noticed that he was drawing flames around that skull. I liked the visual, but I asked Mike why he'd added that touch. "I don't know," he responded. "I just thought he'd look better with flames around his head." And he did, as a matter of fact. (I was vaguely aware at this time of an early-'40s Marvel Super Hero called the Blazing Skull who'd had the same look to his head... but I doubt if Mike had ever heard of him, let alone seen a picture of him.)

And so, almost as quickly as you can read these imperishable paragraphs, the Ghost Rider took on a "look." I'll always regret that, somehow, I didn't ask Mike to add crossed bones as the character's chest symbol. Almost all Super Heroes in those days sported chest symbols, and in this case Ghost Rider would've looked like a walking personification of a skull and crossbones. But I didn't think of it. Also, his "black leather" outfit tended to get left "open for color," so that it generally looked more blue than black.

Gary came strolling in the next day and saw the drawing Mike had done. "Yep," he said. "Just like I pictured it." And it probably was.

From that point I was content to leave the Ghost Rider in the capable hands of Gary and Mike, and they turned it into an instant hit in a comic titled *Marvel Spotlight*. After seven bimonthly issues, Ghost Rider graduated to his own monthly title—*Ghost Rider* #1—with a cover date of September 1973. And he never looked back.

Oh, he's been in and out of his own mag at various times over the past three decades-plus. He began life as a motorcyclist named Johnny Blaze (a name Stan came up with), and later another man took over both the look and the cycle, with some glitzy chains added. Ghost Rider was part of a group of supernatural heroes called the Midnight Sons for a while there, too.

But it all flowed—no sense being modest about it—from what Gary, Mike, and I did, over those few days in 1972.

It's fun to be in on the birth of a comic-book hero who's likely to be around a lot longer than any of us will.

But then, why shouldn't he? He's a ghost, after all!

ROY THOMAS

CHAPTER 1

ORIGINS

THE ORIGINS OF THE GHOST RIDER are buried deep in the annals of history. Long before the pyramids rose above the plains of Egypt, Columbus reached the Americas, and Atlantis sank beneath the oceans, the story of the Ghost Riders begins. It can be dated to a time when humanity was still a fledgling race, struggling for survival in a wild and brutal world. A time when humans were defended by the benevolent Spirits of Vengeance and the enigmatic Blood, and preyed upon by the god-like Zarathos and deceitful Mephisto. It is a story of violent wars and titanic powerplays, in which humans were often little more than the spoils of victory. It is then, over twenty millennia ago, that the story of the Ghost Riders begins.

HISTORY'S VICTIMS
The Ghost Rider legend is a mythic tale of pain, misery, and a terrible curse. As titanic forces of good and evil clashed throughout history, heartache, suffering, and loss were invariably left in their wake.

THE GHOST RIDERS

THE STORY OF the Ghost Riders began thousands of years ago with the Spirits of Vengeance and the ancient Blood, and the silver-tongued Mephisto and the powerful Zarathos. Their titanic struggles would shape the course of humanity's development. Most citizens of earth were oblivious to these conflicts, but over the centuries a small clutch of humans became embroiled. Johnny Blaze and his mother, Naomi, Noble Kale, and Dan Ketch were all destined to become foot soldiers in these awesome battles.

SPIRITS OF VENGEANCE
The Spirits of Vengeance were dedicated to protecting humanity. Beings of awesome power, their strength was matched only by that of the greatest demons.

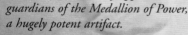

THE BLOOD
The ancient and powerful race known as the Blood were the self-appointed guardians of the Medallion of Power, a hugely potent artifact.

THE MEDALLION OF BLOOD

ZARATHOS AND MEPHISTO
Rivals for dominion over the earth, both Zarathos and Mephisto gained power by feasting on human souls.

THE FIRST GHOST RIDER
Noble Kale was the latest in a long line to inherit a fragment of the Medallion of Power. When Noble's home town was attacked by the Furies, his father chose to sacrifice him. With Mephisto's help, Noble's father combined his son's soul with the essence of the Spirits of Vengeance inside the Medallion, and forged the first Ghost Rider.

THE CURSE
Mephisto's true aim was to take Noble's soul, but Uriel, an angel, prevented him from claiming it. Instead, Noble would live on as the Ghost Rider, and in each generation one of his descendents would host his spirit. The Ghost Rider curse had begun.

NAOMI BLAZE
Naomi Blaze, a descendant of Noble Kale, had three children with her husband, Barton. After inheriting the Ghost Rider curse, she was desperate to save her eldest son from it, and tried to make a bargain with Mephisto.

20,000 BC

• *Zarathos seizes the Medallion of Power, seeking to dominate humanity. The Spirits of Vengeance and the Blood unite to defeat him, but, in one final battle, the Spirits of Vengeance and Zarathos are destroyed and their essence is melded into the Medallion.*

• *The Blood break up the Medallion and place the fragments in two human families. These families are known as the Kales and Badilinos.*

• *Zarathos's body is revived by a desperate tribe and the empowered Zarathos comes to Mephisto's attention. Mephisto defeats Zarathos and enslaves his life essence.*

1700s

• *Noble Kale falls in love with Magdalena, who becomes pregnant. Noble's father is furious and, after the birth, Magdalena is burned at the stake. As she dies Magdalena calls down the Furies to destroy the town.*

• *Noble's father makes a pact with Mephisto—in exchange for his soul, Noble is transformed into the first Ghost Rider.*

1970s

• *Noble Kale's descendent, Naomi Blaze, has three children—Johnny, Barbara, and Dan.*

• *Naomi makes a deal with Mephisto so that Johnny won't become the Ghost Rider and she has her other children adopted.*

• *As she dies, Naomi is told that Johnny won't become the Ghost Rider, but could*

JOHNNY BLAZE

JOHNNY BLAZE
Despite the efforts of his mother, when stunt rider Johnny Blaze sold his soul to Mephisto, he was transformed into a Ghost Rider. While bearing the likeness of the Ghost Rider, Johnny's body would play host to the demon Zarathos, rather than the spirit of Noble Kale.

HAPPY FAMILIES
Johnny managed to rid himself of Zarathos. He married Roxanne Simpson, and they had two children, Craig and Emma. They were happy, but the specter of the Ghost Rider always haunted them.

THE CURSE IS LIFTED
For three centuries, Noble Kale had lived on as the Ghost Rider, forced to share the bodies of his descendants. Plotting to seize the Medallion of Power, the demon Blackheart returned Noble's original body to him and lifted the curse.

NOBLE KALE

OUR ENEMIES ARE UPON US

DAN KETCH

JOHN BLAZE IN HELL
Years later, John Blaze's pact with Mephisto finally caught up with him. Seized by demons he was carried into hell.

GHOST RIDER RETURNS
John Blaze was reunited with his long-lost brother, Dan, who had become the next Ghost Rider.

1970s

• Following the disappearance of his mother and death of his father, Johnny Blaze is adopted by Crash Simpson.

• Crash learns he has cancer, so Johnny sells his soul to Mephisto to cure Crash, but Crash dies in a stunt-riding accident.

• Johnny's body is bound to the demon Zarathos and he becomes a Ghost Rider.

1980s

• Centurious, Zarathos's ancient enemy, returns to take revenge. Centurious's plan to destroy Zarathos backfires and they both become trapped in the Soul Crystal. With Zarathos imprisoned, Johnny Blaze is free of the Ghost Rider.

• Johnny buys the Quentin Carnival. He returns to stunt riding, settles down, and starts a family.

1990s

• Dan Ketch inherits the Ghost Rider curse from his mother, Naomi Blaze, despite being adopted to protect him.

• When his sister, Barbara, is attacked, Dan becomes another Ghost Rider.

• As Ghost Rider, Dan avenges the innocent of New York; he joins forces with his brother Johnny, now John Blaze.

2000s

• Blackheart returns Noble Kale's body to him as part of a plot to obtain the Medallion. Realizing that Blackheart intends to kill him, Noble strikes first. Blackheart is destroyed but Dan Ketch also dies. The Ghost Rider curse is lifted.

• John Blaze is carried into hell and an offer of escape by the angel Malachi turns out to be a deception. John stays in hell.

ZARATHOS

MORE THAN TWENTY millennia ago, in the days before Atlantis, demons walked the earth. Humanity was watched over by powerful but benevolent entities—the Spirits of Vengeance. Another race—the Blood—were guardians of the Medallion of Power, an artefact of awesome strength. For thousands of years, a balance was maintained between the various powers, until the mighty demon Zarathos seized the Medallion of Power, and began to use it in an effort to dominate the planet.

THE MEDALLION
Although undeniably ancient, the origins of the Medallion of Power remain unknown. A source of awesome mystical energies, the power it offers has been coveted by many.

REIGN OF ZARATHOS

Desperate to defeat Zarathos and protect humanity's future, the Spirits of Vengeance and the Blood united. Zarathos was overthrown, but the cost was high—the Spirits of Vengeance were forced to sacrifice themselves. In the ensuing inferno, their essence and that of Zarathos melded with the Medallion.

Zarathos reborn
Revived once more, Zarathos led his devoted followers to glory and conquest. Waging war on their neighboring tribes, this cult of Zarathos sacrificed their enemies at his altar. Feeding on these defeated souls, Zarathos became ever-more powerful. Once again a threat to humanity, he was also attracting the attention of his demonic rival—Mephisto, the Prince of Liars.

Cult of Zarathos
Despite his defeat at the hands of the Spirits of Vengeance, in some small way Zarathos lived on. Deep inside a network of caverns, his stone body slumbered, preserving a tiny fraction of his life energy. Discovered by a desperate tribe struggling for survival, Zarathos was revived. In return for their worship he agreed to lead them to new prosperity.

ON ITS SURFACE IS INSCRIBED THE ANTE-DILUVIAN SPELL WHICH WILL DRAW THE AGENT OF THEIR SALVATION DOWN TO THE MORTAL SPHERE...

THERE, MY CHIEF: *THERE!* THE STONE-GOD SLUMBERS-- AWAITING MY CALL TO AWAKEN!

I SEE IT, KINUTU--AND WHAT I SEE DOES NOT PLEASE ME!

THE LAWS OF OUR FOREFATHERS FORBID THE PRACTICE OF SORCERY! THAT IS WHY THEY BURIED THE TIMEWORK SCROLLS AND CHARMS WHICH YOU DARED TO UNEARTH WITH THAT ACCURSED TOTEM!

Mephisto's pawn

When the Cult of Zarathos defeated his tribe, a young prince was desperate to save his princess from being sacrificed. Climbing the sacred Mount of Meditation, the prince declared he would do anything to spare his beloved. So the demon Mephisto took his soul and sent him to Zarathos's altar, to offer himself in sacrifice. Greedy for more life energies, Zarathos eagerly reached out to consume the young prince's soul.

MEPHISTO'S REVENGE

Zarathos had been tricked—when he reached out to take the prince's soul, he found nothing and began to burn. Struck down by Mephisto, Zarathos's stone body shattered, and Mephisto enslaved his remaining life essence.

Mephisto enjoyed tormenting Zarathos by binding his soul to others. Johnny Blaze was one who suffered this curse.

THE BLOOD AND THE SPIRITS OF VENGEANCE

Even when they walked the earth, the Spirits of Vengeance were mostly creatures of myth, charging into battle, their bodies aflame, striking against their enemies with blazing whips. It is not known why they took such an interest in humans, yet for this seemingly insignificant species, the Spirits made the ultimate sacrifice.

A difficult choice

Following Zarathos's defeat by the Spirits of Vengeance, the Blood faced a difficult choice. As guardians of the Medallion of Power, it was clear that the Medallion was far too dangerous to remain intact.

The Blood break the Medallion into pieces

The Medallion is broken

The Blood placed the fragments of the Medallion into two human families. The eldest children in each generation would inherit the pieces and a Blood called Caretaker would watch over them.

MEPHISTO

THE PRINCE of Liars, a peddler in half-truths and deception, the demon Mephisto was the ruler of a parallel dimension that many on earth consider to be hell. A vengeful demon, Mephisto reveled in the suffering of others, consuming their souls, feasting on their misery, and exulting as he watched them writhe in torment. This vile schemer had strong ties to the human world, where, through bargains and extortion, he would seize the souls of others, leaving behind a trail of misery and mayhem.

> OH, LOOK AT ALL THE PRETTY LITTLE MORTALS PLAYING WITH THE SUPERNATURAL

> M-M-*MEPHISTO!*

Demonic rivals

Following his revival by a desperate tribe, Zarathos quickly came to Mephisto's attention. Zarathos's success in harvesting souls and generating a small army of followers aroused Mephisto's fury—as his might grew, Zarathos was encroaching on Mephisto's territory. It was not long before the demon lord began scheming and plotting ways to overthrow his new rival.

> BUT SUCH POWER CANNOT GO LONG UNNOTICED...

> THIS ZARATHOS DESTROYS SOULS THAT SHOULD BY RIGHTS BELONG TO THE LORDS OF HADES! HE SEEKS A SEA OF FOLLOWERS TO RIVAL OURS, AS WELL!

A NOBLE PLAN

In recent centuries, Mephisto had become increasingly interested in obtaining the Medallion of Power, and he set his sights on one of the families that bore its fragments—the Kales. When his home came under attack from the Furies, the head of the Kale family entreated Mephisto for help. Mephisto agreed to assist him, in return for the soul of his son, Noble.

> SO MY FATHER ONCE AGAIN MADE A DEAL WITH HIS DEVIL... THE DARK LORD MEPHISTO.

GHOST RIDER
Activating the fragment of the Medallion in Noble's blood, Mephisto transformed Noble into a new Spirit of Vengeance—the first Ghost Rider. Noble then drove the Furies away.

SOUL SAVED
When Mephisto tried to collect Noble's soul, he was prevented from doing so by an angelic entity, Uriel. Instead, Noble and his descendents would bear the Ghost Rider curse.

> I'LL TAKE WHATEVER I WANT!

> THIS ABOMINATION WILL NOT COME TO PASS! DO NOT FORCE MY SWORD!

Malevolent trickster

A slippery being, it is hard even to be sure of Mephisto's original name. Sometimes presenting himself as Satan, the devil, he has also been known to take human form and wander inconspicuously among mortals, searching out human prey. Whatever name or form he takes, one thing is certain—Mephisto is truly evil and is not to be trusted.

Treachery

Mephisto's defeat of Zarathos only came about as a result of a bargain struck with a young prince. In return for the prince's soul, Mephisto promised to help him save his princess.

A TERRIBLE SACRIFICE
The prince's bargain with Mephisto had terrible implications. Although he saved his beloved from Zarathos's clutches, by giving up his soul, the prince was no longer able to love her. Cursed with immortality, he adopted the name Centurious. As the years passed he wandered the earth, desperate to fill the great void in his existence.

LOST LOVE
The princess was broken-hearted when Centurious pushed her away. She may have escaped death, but her future was destined to be lonely.

BLAZE BETRAYED
Having inherited the Ghost Rider curse, Naomi Blaze wanted to save her son, Johnny, from the same fate. Mephisto promised Johnny would not become the Ghost Rider. However, he could still become a Ghost Rider.

A bargain broken

Like his mother, Johnny Blaze was also fated to strike a bargain with Mephisto. In return for his soul, Johnny asked that his adopted father, Crash Simpson, should not die of cancer. Mephisto kept his promise, to the letter. Instead of cancer, Crash was killed in a stunt-riding accident a few days later.

NO...

NO!

Mephisto defeated

Despite repeated attempts to seize the Medallion of Power, Mephisto was thwarted at every turn. He employed every ounce of cunning yet still his enemies defeated him. At the same time, new threats to his demonic empire were constantly emerging. Even Mephisto's own son, Blackheart, was envious of his father's power. Unwilling to wait for his inheritance, Blackheart plotted to overthrow Mephisto, and eventually succeeded.

CHAPTER 2

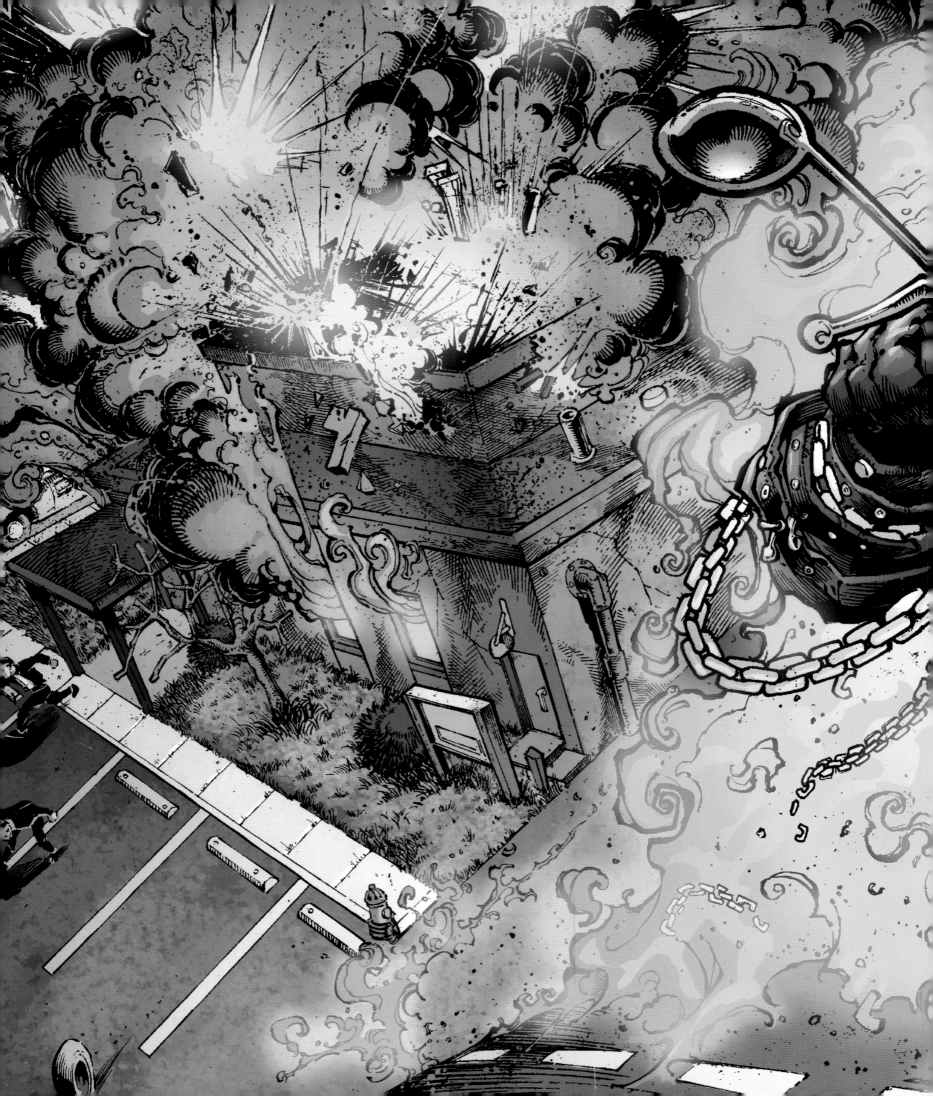

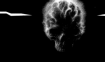

...HNNY BLAZE

... CENTURIES Ghost Riders have stalked
... but it is only recently that they have
...eing figures of popular myth and come
...am attention. This transition began 30
...hen Ghost Rider roamed the byways
... his soul hosted by Johnny Blaze. Born
... with a treacherous demon, this Ghost
...t to avenge the innocent and to right
...ding a motorcycle forged of fire, his
...ll beset by flame, he cast fear into the
...minals and innocent alike. Traveling
... to town, Ghost Rider wielded his
...st countless wrongdoers, searing their
...-visiting their misdeeds upon them.
... he traveled until one day, almost as
...had emerged, he simply disappeared.

IT'S BEGINNING

JOHNNY BLAZE

FROM THE DAY HE WAS BORN, Johnny Blaze was destined to lead the life of a wanderer. The son of traveling stunt riders Barton Blaze and Naomi Kale, Johnny grew up moving from town to town as part of the Crash Simpson Stunt Cycle Spectacular. This itinerant, restless existence was the one sure thing in Johnny's life. Abandoned by his mother at a young age and, a short time later, deprived of his father as the result of a terrible accident, Johnny was doomed to travel continuously.

A stranger visits
The disappearance of his mother and younger siblings was hugely traumatic for the young Johnny Blaze, so he blocked them out of his memory. Over the years, he came to believe that his mother, Naomi, was dead. When she returned to see him some years later, Johnny didn't recognize her, and an angry Crash Simpson forced her to leave.

ORPHANED BY TRAGEDY

When he was still very young, Johnny's mother, Naomi, left home. Taking Johnny's younger sister and brother with her, Naomi left Johnny to be raised by his father, Barton Blaze. For a time all was well, but when Barton was killed in a tragic accident, Johnny was left all alone. Crash Simpson had known John all his life and asked the youngster to move in with him, his wife, Mona, and daughter Roxanne. Together they would be John's new family.

Crash Simpson

Mona Simpson

Johnny Blaze

Roxanne Simpson

Crash Simpson thrills the world
The years following his father's death were the most thrilling of Johnny's life. Continuing to criss-cross the United States with his new family, he learned to ride, and stood in awe of Crash's motorcycling prowess. Years earlier, Crash Simpson had set up his own stunt show and had begun building it up. He was sure fame was just around the corner.

Crash Simpson wows his audience

Death dogs Johnny Blaze
Before Crash and Mona Simpson could enjoy their success, tragedy struck once more. When a rehearsal for a new stunt went wrong, Johnny was forced to leap off his bike to save himself. Rushing to his side, Mona Simpson sustained appalling injuries as the bike collided with a tree and exploded.

PROMISE ME, JOHNNY... PROMISE ME... YOU WILL NEVER... RIDE IN THE SHOW! PLEASE... JOHNNY!

I... PROMISE... MOTHER!

A hard promise to keep

Called to Mona Simpson's bedside, Johnny was the last person to talk to her before she died. Racked with guilt, he listened carefully as Mona made a terrible last request. She asked him to promise to give up the one thing he truly loved. Stunt riding was in Johnny's blood, but Mona wanted him to give it up altogether, and never to ride again in the show. Numb with grief, he made the promise and called her "mother"— something he had long wanted to do.

Roxanne and Johnny finally acknowledge their love

Shoulder to cry on

Johnny and the Simpsons had always been tight-knit, but Mona's death drew them even closer. Kneeling by Mona's grave, Johnny comforted Roxanne.

THE TIES THAT BIND
Roxanne saw her mother's death for what it was—a terrible accident—and did not blame Johnny for what had happened.

Love blossoms

While touring the country was certainly exotic for Johnny and Roxanne Simpson, it was also terribly lonely, and increasingly they turned to each other for support. Perhaps it was inevitable that romance would blossom. Unfortunately, their newfound happiness was to be short-lived. It would not be long before their lives were turned upside down once again.

THE COMING OF THE GHOST RIDER

JOHNNY BLAZE NEVER REALIZED how difficult it would be to keep his promise to the dying Mona Simpson—never to ride again in Crash Simpson's stunt show. While he knew he would miss riding immensely, he didn't foresee the hurt his promise would cause to Crash himself. For years Johnny had been a son to Crash—someone who would one day take over the show—but without Johnny's involvement, all Crash's hopes seemed to be dashed.

TENSIONS RISE
Johnny's promise to Mona had been made just moments before her death and so he chose to keep it to himself. As the years passed, this secrecy increased the tensions between Johnny and Crash.

BRANDED A COWARD

Despite Mona's death and his upset at Johnny's refusal to perform, Crash Simpson continued to pour his energies into the stunt show. Five years on, he was about to hit the big time—a performance at Madison Square Gardens—when he learned he was dying of cancer. Refusing to take over from Crash and continue the business, Johnny was branded a coward by Roxanne.

Secrets revealed

In fact, Roxanne knew that Johnny was no coward. Months earlier, she had seen him stunt riding in secret. While he had promised not to perform in the show, he decided he could still ride for his own enjoyment.

Pact with a devil

Unable to face losing Crash, Johnny attempted to conjure Satan and seek his help, using books on the occult he had secretly been studying. Little did Johnny realize that he had actually summoned the demon Mephisto, a creature with an enduring interest in Johnny and his family. In return for Johnny's soul, Mephisto promised that Crash would not die of cancer.

A bargain betrayed

Crash never learned that his cancer had been cured. At Madison Square Gardens, he decided to die in glory and set up an ambitious stunt—to jump over 22 cars and beat the world record. Believing that his pact would save Crash, Johnny did not try and stop him.

A hero falls

Johnny knew the stunt was too ambitious. Although Mephisto had promised that Crash wouldn't be killed by cancer, that didn't rule out death by motorcycle.

CRASH... OH, LORD... CRRAAASHHH!

A FATHER DIES
Charging across the arena, Johnny was the first to reach Crash Simpson, but it was too late. Racked with remorse, Johnny returned to the arena and successfully completed the jump himself, but it was all for nothing...

Mephisto returns

Determined to enforce their bargain, Mephisto confronted Johnny and demanded his soul. Only Roxanne's intervention saved him. Pure in heart and in love with Johnny, Roxanne was able to drive Mephisto away.

YOU!

YOU DOUBLE-CROSS ME... THEN APPEAR AGAIN! YOU GOT A LOT OF GALL, DEVIL!

SILENCE, WEAKLING! I KEPT MY BARGAIN! THE MORTAL DID NOT DIE OF THE DISEASE! NOW I CLAIM MY REWARD... YOUR VERY SOUL!

NO...

NO!

IT'S ALL RIGHT, DARLING! HE'S GONE... NEVER TO RETURN... AS LONG AS I STAY WITH YOU!

BUT... I DON'T UNDERSTAND! HOW DID YOU KNOW...?!

Zarathos bound

Roxanne's love could not save Johnny altogether. Still having some control over him, Mephisto used Johnny's body as a host for the demon Zarathos. That night, Johnny was transformed into a figure with a blazing skull. The Ghost Rider had arrived.

NOOOOOOOOOO

CRASH SIMPSON

ALL HIS LIFE Crash Simpson had dreamed of running his own motorcycle stunt show. For years he had scrimped, saved, and struggled. Then, just as he was about to hit the big time, Crash learned he had cancer. Although he was miraculously cured, Crash died anyway when a motorcycle stunt went wrong. When Mephisto offered him a second chance at life, Crash seized the opportunity. But there was a terrible catch—Crash had to sacrifice his adopted son, Johnny Blaze.

A LONG, LONG ROAD
Starting out as a motorcycle cop, Crash Simpson went on to work at the Quentin Carnival before setting up his own stunt show.

CURLY SAMUELS

Returning to Earth, Crash Simpson was given the body of Curly Samuels, the head of a New York motorcycling gang, Satan's Servants. It was not long before Crash encountered Johnny Blaze, traveling the streets as Ghost Rider, desperate for somewhere to rest. When he was invited to stay with the gang, Johnny agreed.

NAME'S *CURLY...CURLY SAMUELS!* I *RUN* THE GANG...AND WE COULD USE A *FAR-OUT JOCK* LIKE YOU!

THAT IS, IF YOU'LL CUT THE *MUMBO-JUMBO* AND CLUE ME *IN!*

A NEW BODY
Despite the curly red wig, Crash felt comfortable in his new body.

Second time lucky
Better prepared second time around, Crash stripped to the waist, placed Ghost Rider in the center of a mystical pentagram, raised a sheep's skull into the air, and began a series of incantations. Sure enough, after a short time, Mephisto's sinister presence could be felt.

FINALLY, THE SYMBOL IS PAINTED ON THE *FLOOR*-- AND MY HUMAN SACRIFICE LIES IN THE *CENTER* OF IT!

NOW...I RECITE THE SACRED *INCANTATION...*

THROUGH THE *ETERNAL* THROUGH ENDLESS *SPACE*, I *BEG* THEE *JOURNEY* TO THIS PLACE!

HEAR ME, OH DIVINE MASTER OF DARKNESS AND EVIL! IF YOU ARE *PLEASED...* APPEAR AND LET ME *KNOW* OF YOUR PLEASURE.

MORE HASTE, LESS SPEED
Placing Ghost Rider in a trance, Crash's first attempt to contact Mephisto failed because he had not prepared fully.

Final demand
Returning to his true form, Crash prepared to speak to Mephisto. What he was told tested his character to the limits...

AS LONG AS HER LOVE IS HIS...I CANNOT *POSSESS* HIS *SOUL!* THERE-FORE...IT IS UP TO YOU TO REMOVE THIS *BARRIER!*

BUT...SHE IS...MY *DAUGHTER!*

ROXANNE SIMPSON

THROUGHOUT HER CHILDHOOD, death had shadowed Roxanne Simpson. Following the death of Barton Blaze in a tragic accident, Roxanne suffered the loss of her own mother, Mona. Five years on, her father, Crash, also died. From that point, Roxanne's life would never be settled. Although she had brief periods of happiness, Roxanne was destined to suffer on the sidelines as her soulmate, Johnny Blaze, fought endless battles with mystical forces.

Crash's quandary

When offered Johnny Blaze's body, Mephisto was unable to extract the young man's soul. As long as Roxanne Simpson was alive, Johnny was protected.

YOU DIDN'T SCARE ME *LAST NIGHT,* FREAK FACE... AND YOU SURE DON'T SCARE ME *NOW!*

JOHNNY! MY LORD...IS IT *YOU?!*

BUT YOUR FOE WILL FIGHT YOU AS YOU *WERE...* SO THAT THE *SHOCK* OF YOUR TRUE IDENTITY MAY OFFSET THE ADVANTAGE OF HIS *POWERS!*

GOOD LORD! CURLEY'S --*CHANGING!*

CHANGING INTO-- *CRASH SIMPSON!* BUT HE'S *DEAD!*

HIGH PRICE TO PAY

To be reborn into his own body once more, Crash Simpson had to sacrifice his daughter, Roxanne. So, he transported both Roxanne and Ghost Rider to Mephisto's realm. Once there, Ghost Rider refused to die quietly, launching a desperate fight for survival. As their battle escalated, Crash finally came to his senses and turned on Mephisto. Determined to protect the two people he loved most in the world, Crash sacrificed his own life to keep them safe.

SACRIFICIAL VICTIM
The trauma Roxanne suffered in Mephisto's realm did not cause her lasting harm. Despite waking up in Johnny's arms, unusually dressed, Roxanne passed off the events as a dream. She would never know how close her father had come to killing her.

Soulmates divided...

After the death of her father, Roxanne's relationship with Johnny became more difficult. When the stunt show was forced to close, she followed him to Hollywood, but the pressure of his double life drove her to leave him. It did not take Roxanne long to realize that she could not live without Johnny. However, before she could find him, Roxanne's memories were wiped by the criminal named Orb.

LOOK AT ME ROXANNE SIMPSON!

LOOK AT ME!

I MISSED YOU.

CRAIG, EMMA, ALL OF YOU!

... and reunited

Years later, Johnny and Roxanne were reunited. Freed from the Ghost Rider, they got married and had two children. For a time, they were happy, but it did not last. When the demon biker returned, the consequences for Roxanne would be dire...

JOHNNY BLAZE'S POWERS

JOHNNY BLAZE WAS ALREADY a brilliant stunt rider. Following his transformation into Ghost Rider, he also became virtually indestructible. With heightened reflexes, he was now able to take risks that would terrify others. However, it was not just his motorcycling skills that had been enhanced. Boasting formidable strength and the ability to project hellfire from his hands, Johnny was more than able to battle wrongdoers and mystical forces. Often just his appearance was enough to make his enemies retreat.

JOHNNY BLAZE VS. GHOST RIDER

At first, Johnny Blaze seemed able to control the Ghost Rider. Although his appearance would change, Johnny was still the same man underneath and he could always remember what he had done in his demonic form. However, Ghost Rider gradually became a more forceful presence and as Johnny's hold weakened, the brimstone biker became increasingly vengeful and violent.

Hellfire and damnation
It wasn't just Ghost Rider's skull that blazed with hellfire, he could also project it from his hands. It could be fired as blasts of energy or used to seer the souls of his enemies, forcing them to suffer the terrible torments they had meted out to others. So horrifying was this experience that some of Ghost Rider's victims committed suicide.

FIREWALL
With a gesture, Ghost Rider could create a wall of flames, trapping his enemies until the authorities arrived.

FLAME-BIKE

To begin with, Ghost Rider battled his enemies on Johnny Blaze's stunt bike. It was only when stranded in the desert that he learned how to create a bike out of hellfire. Much more powerful than an ordinary motorcycle, the flame-bike became Ghost Rider's new vehicle of choice.

MUSCLEMAN
He may be all bone and hellfire, but Ghost Rider possesses superhuman strength. He can even pick up grown men and hurl them across a room.

Taking control

At first, Johnny could not control the timing of his agonizing transformation into Ghost Rider, and every night as the sun went down, the demon biker would emerge. Later this pattern changed, and the transformation would only occur when danger was nearby. In time, Johnny learned how to prevent it from happening and could even trigger the change.

JOHNNY'S MOTORCYCLE

HIS HEAD WREATHED IN FLAME, Ghost Rider struck fear into the hearts of innocent and evil alike. His motorcycle, with its flaming wheels, made him a truly intimidating figure. Without the bike's sinister, throbbing purr echoing down the streets of night to herald his arrival, the hearts of miscreants across America would not have beat and raced with the same rapidity, and Ghost Rider's presence would have menaced all the less. Whether sitting astride Johnny Blaze's original chopper, or racing on a bike fashioned from hellfire itself, Ghost Rider and his bike were intrinsically linked.

CONTROLLING THE VERTICAL

Bound to the body of the world's greatest stunt rider, Ghost Rider could draw on Johnny Blaze's uncanny riding ability, and perform motorcycling feats that would cause even the most confident riders to stop, draw breath, and think twice. In part, this was because his motorcycle was powered by dark and unnatural powers, which enabled him to do the physically impossible, such as charging up vertical surfaces.

FLAME BIKE
To begin with, Ghost Rider simply rode Johnny Blaze's bike. Later, he learned to forge his own motorcycle out of hellfire. Called the flame bike, this fiery steed was even more powerful than Johnny's own stunt cycle.

Like Johnny's stunt cycle, the flame bike was also a chopper, the trident at its rear signifying its arcane origins

ALMOST NOTHING IS IMPOSSIBLE FOR *JOHN BLAZE* TO ACCOMPLISH ON A *MOTORCYCLE.*

AND WITH THE RECENT ACQUISITION OF A MYSTICALLY POWERED MOTORCYCLE...

... EVEN THE IMPOSSIBLE HAS BECOME *POSSIBLE.*

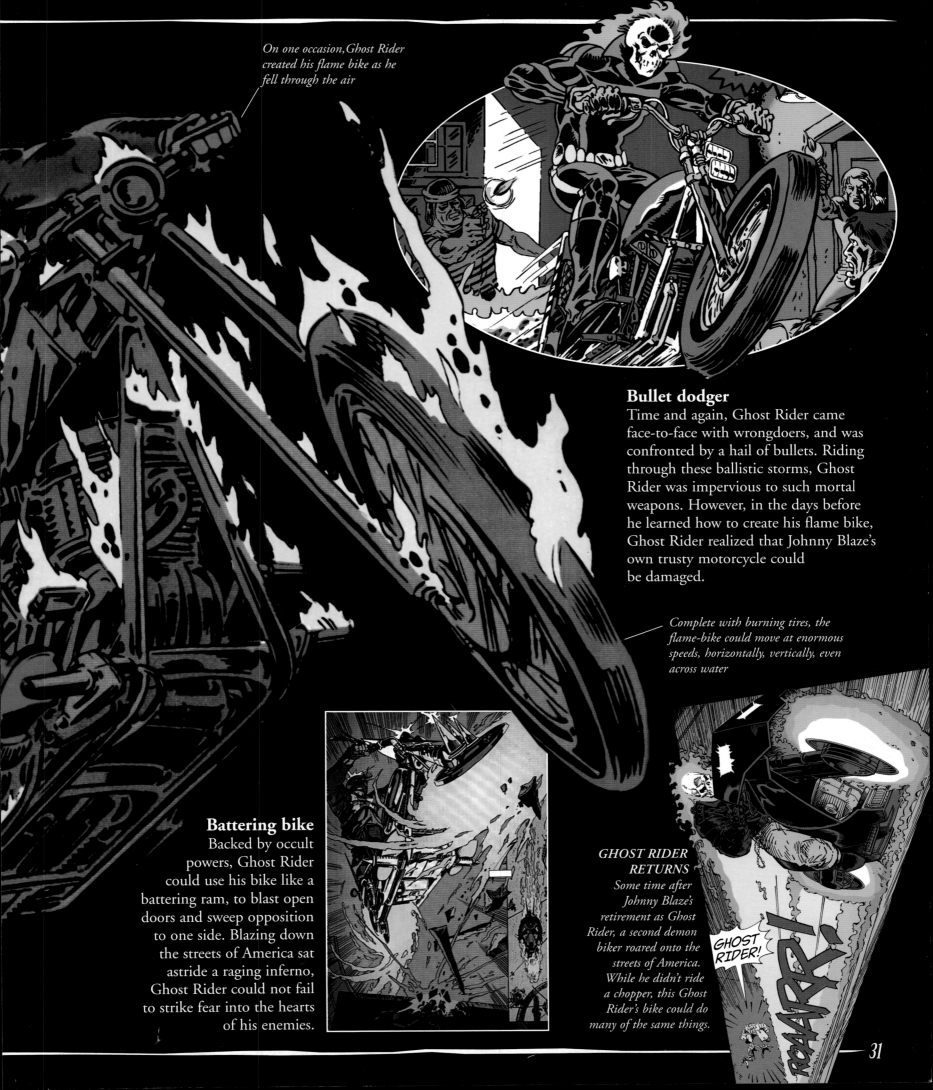

On one occasion, Ghost Rider created his flame bike as he fell through the air

Bullet dodger

Time and again, Ghost Rider came face-to-face with wrongdoers, and was confronted by a hail of bullets. Riding through these ballistic storms, Ghost Rider was impervious to such mortal weapons. However, in the days before he learned how to create his flame bike, Ghost Rider realized that Johnny Blaze's own trusty motorcycle could be damaged.

Complete with burning tires, the flame-bike could move at enormous speeds, horizontally, vertically, even across water

Battering bike

Backed by occult powers, Ghost Rider could use his bike like a battering ram, to blast open doors and sweep opposition to one side. Blazing down the streets of America sat astride a raging inferno, Ghost Rider could not fail to strike fear into the hearts of his enemies.

GHOST RIDER RETURNS

Some time after Johnny Blaze's retirement as Ghost Rider, a second demon biker roared onto the streets of America. While he didn't ride a chopper, this Ghost Rider's bike could do many of the same things.

GHOST RIDER!

ROARR!

31

COPPERHEAD CANYON

HAVING INHERITED CRASH SIMPSON'S stunt show, Johnny Blaze and Roxanne left New York and headed to the American Midwest where Johnny was to star in the local rodeo and attempt a new feat of bravery—a leap across the nearby Copperhead Canyon. Little did he realize that this visit would put him in the middle of a bitter land dispute. The local American Indians, desperate to establish their claim on the area, did not relish the publicity Johnny Blaze would bring and were determined to stop him.

INDIAN RESERVATION
A daredevil leap across Copperhead Canyon would bring John some much-valued publicity, but could he overcome the objections of the local Apache tribe?

IT'S *GAINING* ON ME! HAVE TO GET AWAY FROM *IT*... OR FROM THE BRAIN THAT'S *CREATING* IT!

GHOST RIDER TAKES A FALL

Despite the opposition he was facing, Johnny was still determined to jump Copperhead Canyon. While heading into the desert, he was attacked by the witch doctor Snakedance. As Ghost Rider, he fought off the first attacks, but when Snakedance transformed into a giant serpent, Ghost Rider was forced to flee. Running out of road he leapt off the edge of the canyon, but then his bike exploded...

WHROOM!

Ghost Rider indestructible
His body crushed on the rocks, Johnny's end seemed nigh. Then Mephisto appeared—still wearing the guise of Satan. Ghost Rider would not be allowed to die, Johnny was told, until Mephisto had gained possession of his soul.

Human sacrifice

With Johnny Blaze out of the way, Snakedance and his fellow tribesmen kidnapped Roxanne. Their Serpent-God had demanded a human sacrifice—someone to become the god's bride—and it was to be Roxanne. Binding Roxanne to a ceremonial tree, the tribe performed an exotic ceremony. At its climax, the poisoned fangs of two copperhead snakes bit into her wrists. Although Ghost Rider arrived just minutes later, Roxanne's life was already ebbing away. Only expert medics could save her.

Linda to the rescue

With the hospital so far away, the chance of Roxanne surviving seemed slim. Fortunately, Snakedance's daughter, Linda Littletree, managed to obtain a healing serum.

Linda Littletree was an excellent shot. Combined with her academic success, this had earned her the tribe's respect.

WHAT SHOULD I *CALL* YOU--? *JOHNNY BLAZE? GHOST RIDER?!* LITTLE *DIFFERENCE* IT MAKES--

--SINCE YOU NOW ARE IN THE HANDS OF *WITCH-WOMAN*--

--WHOSE INTENTION IT IS TO DELIVER YOUR SOUL TO ITS RIGHTFUL OWNER-- *SATAN!!*

LINDA LITTLETREE
Linda's arrival stunned the tribe back to its senses. Having just returned from college, Linda scolded them for their stupidity— if Roxanne died, the authoriries would become involved and heir future would be doomed anyway.

Pawn of Mephisto

It soon emerged that there was more to Linda Littletree than first appeared. While at college, Linda was tricked into becoming a servant of Mephisto. Her return to Copperhead Canyon was no coincidence—she had been commanded to destroy Johnny Blaze, although Roxanne was to be allowed to live. Despite Linda's determined efforts, Ghost Rider refused to die. Instead, with the aid of Daimon Hellstrom, Ghost Rider managed to reclaim Linda's soul from Mephisto.

THE CHAMPIONS

DURING HIS TRAVELS AS

Ghost Rider, Johnny Blaze occasionally fought alongside other Super Heroes, but only once did he join a Super Hero team. The Champions first came together to help the Olympian deity Hercules defeat Pluto, the God of the Underworld. Johnny Blaze, the mutants Angel and Iceman, the ex-Russian spy Black Widow, and Hercules then decided to form the first West Coast Super Hero team.

ONWARD, MY COMRADES! THE TIME HAS COME TO FACE OUR *GREATEST FOES!*

ANGEL

HERCULES

GHOST RIDER

FINANCIAL BACKER
Following the death of his parents, Angel inherited a vast fortune and decided to use it to bankroll the Champions.

UNLIKELY TEAM

Nothing ever went to plan for the Champions. Although Angel had styled them as "heroes for the common man," the group's enemies were the usual motley assortment of superpowered criminals. The group also failed to gel. Although they had some successes, including defeating the Crimson Dynamo and Rampage—with the help of Swarm, Lord of the Killer Bees—the group continued to bicker.

34

BLACK WIDOW

ICEMAN

YOUR COMRADES CANNOT *HELP* YOU, HERCULES!

TODAY BELONGS TO **PLUTO, GOD** OF **HELL!**

Trapped on Olympus

The Greek God Pluto first brought the Champions together. In a plot to overthrow Zeus, Pluto captured Hercules and Venus, took them to Olympus, and tried to force them into marrying his allies. Once wed, they would be prevented from defending Zeus when Pluto attacked him. The soon-to-be Champions followed Pluto and exposed his scheme.

DARKSTAR
The Russian mutant Darkstar had the power to manipulate the Dark Force, a mysterious energy field. At first an enemy of the Champions, she later joined them but never truly gained their trust.

Rampage

When Stuart Clarke's company went bankrupt, he renamed himself Rampage and used one of his inventions—an exo-skeleton—to rob banks. He was foiled by the Champions.

STUNT-MASTER

Reformed villain Stunt-Master was a stunt man and actor. While assisting Johnny Blaze in his battle with the villainous Zodiak, Stunt-Master came to admire Johnny's motorcycling skills and offered him work in Hollywood. Johnny was only able to take up the offer when he had gained control of his transformations into Ghost Rider.

I WANT YOU TO MEET MY CO-STAR, KAREN PAGE.

KAREN PAGE
Johnny was introduced to his co-star, Karen Page. Daredevil Matt Murdock's former girlfriend, Karen had decided to try her hand as an actress.

Hot property

By the time Johnny Blaze arrived in Hollywood, Stunt-Master was becoming frustrated with his work. As a star, he was no longer allowed to perform stunts, leaving an opening for a new stunt man.

AND BRING HER TO DEATH'S-HEAD!

Death's-Head

Stunt-Master's relationship with Johnny was tested by the villainous Death's-Head. Death's-Head hypnotized Stunt-Master and forced him to kidnap Karen Page and take her to his hideout. Johnny was furious, but the friendship survived when Stunt-Master helped find Karen.

THE WILDERNESS YEARS

JOHNNY BLAZE HAD GROWN UP traveling from town to town, never settling, always the nomad. After closing down his stunt show, Johnny tried to put down roots in Hollywood, where he worked as a studio stunt man. Although happy for a time, Johnny gradually got itchy feet. Over time he and Roxanne had drifted apart, so when she began dating a studio lackey, he left Los Angeles altogether. Although Johnny had a series of romances, no one ever matched up to Roxanne.

Gina Langtree
When Johnny Blaze was mugged on a freight train, he suffered memory loss and was taken in by Gina Langtree, a racing car test driver. Finding Johnny attractive, she hired him as a mechanic, but their relationship fell apart when Gina discovered his demonic alter ego.

KAREN PAGE
Hollywood starlet Karen Page had previously worked as Matt Murdock's secretary. Also at one time Matt's lover, Karen was the only person to know that he was really the Super Hero Daredevil. Karen was attracted to Johnny Blaze when he started work at Delazny Studios. However, their fledgling relationship petered out after Roxanne Simpson's return and it became obvious where Johnny's affections truly lay.

UNITED STATES

Negura•
NEVADA

Denver•
COLORADO

 Hollywood
CALIFORNIA

Katy Milner
Katy Milner was Karen Page's stunt double. For a time a love triangle existed between Katy, Karen, and Johnny Blaze. Katy had been possessed by one of Mephisto's servants, and when Daimon Hellstrom drove the demon out, Katy's true form was revealed—Roxanne Simpson!

TABICANTRA

Tabicantra was a servant of the demon Azmodeus, sent from the netherworld to destroy Johnny Blaze. Her orders were to make Johnny change into Ghost Rider several times in succession. Weakened by these transformations he would eventually lose the ability to regain his human form. The plan went wrong when Tabicantra fell in love with Johnny, and sacrificed herself to save his life.

THE MIDWEST

OF AMERICA

Chicago •
ILLINOIS

Round Robin •
PENNSYLVANIA

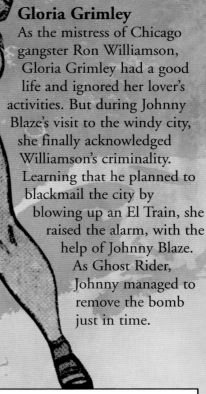

Gloria Grimley

As the mistress of Chicago gangster Ron Williamson, Gloria Grimley had a good life and ignored her lover's activities. But during Johnny Blaze's visit to the windy city, she finally acknowledged Williamson's criminality. Learning that he planned to blackmail the city by blowing up an El Train, she raised the alarm, with the help of Johnny Blaze. As Ghost Rider, Johnny managed to remove the bomb just in time.

Sally Stanton

Johnny Blaze first encountered Sally Stanton one stormy night. Finding her by the roadside, Johnny stopped to offer her a lift. He quickly became drawn into her tragic story—Sally was a ghost, killed years earlier by a drunk driver. She had returned to help her mother move on. By the time Johnny left Pennsylvania, Sally's mother was a happier person.

DEBBIE

A sweet girl, Debbie worked as a dancer in a run-down bar and grill in Denver, Colorado. She barely made a living, and all her earnings were used to pay for her sister's kidney treatment. Debbie gave special attention to Johnny Blaze and the other barflies became jealous and attacked him. When Johnny transformed into Ghost Rider to defend himself, Debbie got scared and asked him to leave her alone—ruining any chance of a relationship.

THE ORB

THE STORY OF THE VILE CRIMINAL known as the Orb is bound up with that of the Simpson family. When Roxanne Simpson's father, Crash, first launched his cycle show he didn't do it on his own but in partnership with one Drake Shannon. Before long, creative differences emerged between the pair, but neither man was willing to give up their share of the show. Eventually, they agreed to a motorcycle cross-country race in which the winner would take all.

SUPERNATURAL ORB

Having lost the race, Drake became withdrawn. Only the intervention of a mysterious group brought Drake back to himself. Equipping him with a spherical mask capable of emitting blasts of energy, the group transformed Drake into the Orb. Driven to take his revenge on the Simpson family, the Orb kidnapped Roxanne, only to be defeated by the combined might of Ghost Rider and Spider-Man.

The race turns dirty
Attempting to run Crash off the road, Drake lost control of his bike. As his body scuttered across the tarmac, his face was damaged horrifyingly.

The Orb cut a fearsome figure with a giant lidless eyeball for a head!

Orb gets kitted out
Despite repeated defeats at Ghost Rider's hands, the Orb never gave up. Determined to bring down his enemy, he upgraded his weaponry. As well as emitting violent blasts of energy, his mask could now fire explosive missiles too. Unsurprisingly, even this ballistic weapon was no match for the brimstone biker.

VENGEANCE WILL NOT OUT
Following their final confrontation, Ghost Rider, tired of the Orb's violent ways, left him stranded in the desert to die under a blazing sun.

An accident in surgery

Shot down in Vietnam, Peter was flown to a hospital ship. There, the surgeons decided to use an experimental device designed to stimulate his cells. However, a power surge during the procedure altered Peter's entire physiognomy.

THE WATER WIZARD

PETER VAN ZANTE MAY HAVE served in Vietnam, but he was still something of an innocent. Despite acquiring the ability to manipulate water, Peter did nothing with this gift until the man known as Mole persuaded him to use it for criminal ends. Peter was ridiculously overconfident and, if he hadn't used his gift against the Ghost Rider, his criminal career would probably have lasted longer than it did.

WATER WORKS
Recovering from the operation, Peter found he was now able to manipulate water.

ENTER THE ENFORCER

Following his first criminal act for the Mole—a bank raid—Peter was approached by the Enforcer, California's would-be kingpin of crime. Now calling himself the Water Wizard, Peter was offered a million dollars to defeat Ghost Rider. Peter did not realize just how powerful the Ghost Rider was and naïvely accepted the offer. Able to destroy water monsters with a burst of hellfire, Ghost Rider was no minor foe.

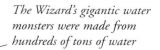
The Wizard's gigantic water monsters were made from hundreds of tons of water

I'LL SHOW THIS *ENFORCER* I'M TOUGH!

MONSTER! KILL THE *GHOST RIDER!*

The water monster cometh!

Following their first encounter, the Wizard struck against Ghost Rider again. Soon the demon biker realized that once the Wizard was disabled, his water monsters disappeared.

HELLFIRE VS WATER
Tiring of the Water Wizard, Ghost Rider hit him with a blast of hellfire. Mentally unbalanced by the violence of the attack, the Wizard was committed to a sanatorium.

FLAGG FARGO

AS JOHNNY BLAZE continued his travels across North America, he left his stunt career further and further behind, and his title—World's Greatest Stunt Rider—up for grabs. There being no shortage of ambitious young stunt riders out there, it was only a matter of time before someone arrived to claim the title, and that someone was Flagg Fargo.

FARGO'S CHALLENGE
Watching Fargo on TV, Blaze was astonished when the young upstart challenged him to a competition.

Fargo accused
Frustrated by his repeated defeats, Johnny became convinced that Fargo was behind the crooks' activities—after all, they were most active during the competition, when the town was deserted. Bursting into Flagg's trailer, Ghost Rider wrongly accused him of treachery.

I'D QUIT DAYDREAMIN' OVER LAST NIGHT'S SCORES AND START WORRYIN' ABOUT TONIGHT IF I WAS YOU, BLAZE! 'CAUSE LAST NIGHT I WAS FEELIN' GENEROUS BUT TONIGHT I MAY JUST DECIDE TO SHUT YOU OUT!

YOU'VE GOT A BIG MOUTH, FARGO! REAL BIG!

BATTLE IS JOINED
Johnny accepted Fargo's challenge, which was to take place over three nights. As the competition began, Ghost Rider became embroiled with some local crooks. Out of practice and exhausted by Ghost Rider's activities, Johnny lost the first two rounds by big margins. Goaded by the arrogant Fargo, the pair almost came to blows.

WE BELIEVED IN YOU, BLAZE! WE EVEN PUT OUR HARD-EARNED BUCKS ON YOU! BUT IN THE END, ALL YOU TURNED OUT TO BE WAS A WORTHLESS HAS-BEEN CREEP!

NO! YOU'RE WRONG!

BLAZING FANS
Initially hesitant about Fargo's challenge, some local barflies persuaded Johnny to accept it, even buying him a new stunt bike.

ALL MY LIFE, BLAZE, EVER SINCE I WAS KID, ALL I EVER WANTED WAS TO BE THE BEST STUNT-RIDER IN THE WHOLE WORLD! AND UNTIL TODAY, WELL, I THOUGHT I WAS!

Johnny redeems himself
By the third day of the competition, Johnny was a long way behind his rival. However, after a stunt riding tour de force, he wowed the crowds and even Fargo himself. Sadly, it was too late—Johnny Blaze had lost his crown.

AZMODEUS

AZMODEUS, THE HIGH LORD OF EVIL, had ambitions to challenge Mephisto. He dreamed of enslaving Ghost Rider, but first he needed to destroy Johnny Blaze. Forcing Blaze to make frequent transformations into Ghost Rider was the way to accomplish this, as it would weaken his ability to regain his human form. Azmodeus and his servant, Tabicantra, focused on this aim.

THIS IS THE HELL-FIRE DEMON WHO WILL BE YOUR ADVERSARY IN THE EARTHLY REALM, TABICANTRA! FOR IT IS HE, KNOWN TO THIS WORLD OF MORTAL MEN AS THE GHOST RIDER, WHOM I WOULD MAKE MY PAWN IN A CAMPAIGN OF FIERY TERROR AGAINST THE EARTH!

TABICANTRA
From the outset, the alluring Tabicantra was attracted to Johnny Blaze, but understood that her true loyalties still lay with her master. Despite this, she couldn't help admiring Johnny's boyish innocence, his heroism, and his daring. Tabicantra was smitten.

WHAT THE BLAZES?

Ignoring her feelings for Johnny, Tabicantra focused on the task of destroying him. She caused him to transform three times: once she forced a bridge to collapse as he crossed it, and another time she attacked him with a demon. Greatly weakened, Johnny was on the brink of annihilation when Tabicantra decided she couldn't see him die.

JOHNNY? LOOK--!!

HOLY CHRISTMAS! I DON'T KNOW WHAT THE HECK IS GOING ON AROUND HERE! BUT I SURE DO KNOW ONE THING! JOHNNY BLAZE WOULDN'T STAND A SNOWBALL'S CHANCE AGAINST THOSE MONSTRO-SITIES--

SACRIFICED
Realizing that his servant had turned traitor, Azmodeus sent demons to attack Johnny Blaze and force one final transformation. Protecting Johnny with a force globe, Tabicantra sacrificed herself.

Azmodeus's downfall

Still eager to enslave Ghost Rider, Azmodeus approached Mephisto and offered to take control of the brimstone biker. Amused, Mephisto suggested that Azmodeus could have Ghost Rider, if the demon biker could beat Johnny Blaze in a race through hell. When Ghost Rider and Blaze eventually drew, Azmodeus received the ultimate punishment—annihilation.

--BUT *OTHER* MATTERS OF IMPORT--AWAIT ME IN MY OWN F-FAR DISTANT REALM!

AS YOU KNOW--I, TOO, HAVE A K-K-K-KINGDOM TO ATTEND TO!

THE ONLY KINGDOM FIT FOR YOUR RULE, ASMODEUS--

--IS *OBLIVION!*

QUENTIN CARNIVAL

OUT OF MONEY and finally ready to settle down, Johnny's journeys across America brought him to the Quentin Carnival, a traveling circus that reminded Johnny of his early life. After showing off his skills, he got a job as the carnival's chief stunt rider. Little did he know that, many years before, his parents and Crash Simpson had worked as stunt riders at the very same carnival.

LATE FOR THE SHOW
As Ghost Rider, Johnny also continued to battle local miscreants. To avoid missing a show he was often forced to race back on his flame bike.

Quentin's secret

Ralph Quentin was haunted by a dark secret. Years earlier, starting out as a carnival owner, a younger, brasher Quentin treated his employees harshly, causing some to die from stress.

Cynthia Randolph

Arriving at the carnival just before Johnny Blaze, Cynthia Randolph was a journalist looking to write a story about traveling with a circus. Her time with the carnival put her in danger's way, time and again.

Although she often denied it, Cynthia Randolph secretly carried a torch for Johnny Blaze

GHOSTIE GOES BERSERK

During his time with the carnival, Johnny Blaze's relationship with Ghost Rider became uneasy and unpredictable. In the early days he could control the Rider's actions, but as the years passed Johnny's influence over the brimstone biker waned. Increasingly, he could not even remember what his violent alter ego had been up to.

Fowler in the red

Following Johnny's arrival, Red Fowler was quickly demoted from chief stunt rider to assistant. This led to tensions between him and Johnny. Unknown to anyone, Red Fowler was seriously in debt to a malevolent money lender called Loan Shark. When Fowler failed to pay, Loan Shark planned to dump him out at sea. Only the arrival of Johnny Blaze saved Fowler's life. Hugely grateful for what Johnny had done, the two became firm friends and a great stunt riding team from that moment on.

I NEED MORE TIME!

YOUR TIME'S UP, YOU WORTHLESS DEADBEAT!

A new stunt partnership

During his run-in with Loan Shark, Red Fowler witnessed Johnny's transformation into Ghost Rider. Thankful to Johnny for rescuing him, Fowler vowed to keep his secret, which helped to cement their partnership.

It took some time for Johnny and Red to perfect their act

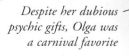

ELIOT THE CLOWN
For years a member of the Circus of Crime, Eliot the Clown returned to the Quentin Carnival following the Circus's escape from prison. Although the Circus of Crime pursued him—even capturing Johnny Blaze—Eliot laid a trap that resulted in their recapture.

Madam Olga

The carnival's medium, Madam Olga, was treated with affection by her fellow carnies. After purchasing a medieval bowl candle, Olga was tricked into releasing an evil spirit—Clothilde. If it wasn't for Ghost Rider's intervention, this being would have caused untold devastation.

Despite her dubious psychic gifts, Olga was a carnival favorite

The Great Vicenzo

One of its longest-serving members, the Great Vincenzo was the carnival magician. During his capture by the criminal Freakmaster, Vincenzo's brain was operated upon, causing him to develop psychic and telepathic gifts. Although he was given the ability to sense danger, Vincenzo's ordeal turned him into a nervous wreck.

CENTURIOUS

THOUSANDS OF YEARS AGO, during his struggle with Zarathos, the demon Mephisto made a bargain with a prince. This proud, decent man was the leader of a tribe conquered by the Cult of Zarathos. Selling his soul to Mephisto in return for the power to defeat Zarathos and save his princess, the prince did not comprehend the price he was paying. Following Zarathos's overthrow, the prince discovered that he could no longer love, nor feel, nor even die.

ZARATHOS FALLS
Zarathos's defeat came when he tried to seize the prince's non-existent soul.

CENTURIOUS WANDERS

Taking the name Centurious, the prince began wandering the earth, and the link to his human side become ever-more tenuous. In ancient Egypt he was introduced to the arcane arts. Learning to extract the souls of others, he stole a Soul Crystal so that he could store their life-essences. Continuing his journeys, Centurious's memories of his origins dimmed, until an encounter with Ghost Rider reawakened them.

Soul destroying
Deep in the swamps of Louisiana, Centurious occupied an old, decaying house. There, a macabre pantomime took place as Centurious played host to his victims—human vessels whose souls had been consumed.

GHOSTIE MAKES GOOD
Revolted by what he saw, Ghost Rider battled Centurious, destroying the house and freeing those imprisoned there.

44

AND YOU HAVE ARRIVED JUST IN TIME FOR A SOOTHING DRINK, AND PERHAPS A GAY DANCE OR TWO!

THE FIRM
Centurious was still to take a full corporeal form following Ghost Rider's destruction of the Stygians. He established the Firm, an organization bent on the destruction of his old enemy.

Down with Centurious
When Centurious realized that Ghost Rider was Zarathos, he set a trap for his old enemy and the pair battled once again. After a desperate struggle, Zarathos and Centurious became trapped in the Soul Crystal.

THE ESCAPING SPIRITS SUCCESSFULLY RESIST.

THE SOULLESS MAN—IS NOT SO LUCKY!

WELCOME MRS. KETCH!

I'M SO PLEASED YOU COULD JOIN US FOR OUR CEREMONIES.

AND HOW ARE YOU TONIGHT MY DEAR?

IN LOVING MEMORY FOR JOY

R.I.P. STEVE BIASI

The Stygian Church
Years later, Centurious managed to escape while binding Zarathos's essence inside the Soul Crystal. Weakened, and unwilling to make his presence known, Centurious hid, and was fed the life essences of desperate, lonely individuals, gathered together by his loyal servants in the Stygian Church.

CENTURIOUS STRIKES
Increasingly powerful, Centurious remained determined to defeat Ghost Rider. Creating an army of superpowered beings, he prepared to make a direct strike.

NIGHTMARE
Nightmare, ruler of an empire of dreams, was an arch manipulator who toyed with all who passed through his realm. Knowing that the terror of nightmares would be magnified if the brimstone biker had his freedom, Nightmare tried to release Ghost Rider from Johnny Blaze.

Memories unlocked
Nightmare contacted Ghost Rider in the Void, where he resided when not occupying Johnny Blaze's body. By unlocking his memories, Nightmare revealed that Ghost Rider was in fact the demon Zarathos.

Attacking Blaze
Nightmare attempted to free Ghost Rider from his human host by destroying Johnny Blaze's self-belief through a series of terrible dreams. When Mona Simpson's spirit intervened, Nightmare was defeated.

A TOWN CALLED HOLLY

IN THE YEARS FOLLOWING her separation from Johnny Blaze, Roxanne Simpson had taken stock of her life. She had lost everything—her parents, her lover, and her life in a traveling show. Lonely and lost, she turned to her only remaining family, her mother's sister, Ida, who was living in a town called Holly. For a time, life in Holly was good for Roxanne, but then the Sin Eater appeared...

Friends reunited
Roxanne asked Johnny to come and help the people of Holly. As they began their four-day journey, they slowly and tentatively revived their old friendship.

THE SIN EATER

When Holly's shy and retiring pastor renamed himself the Sin Eater, life in the sleepy Midwest backwater began to change. Promising to consume their sins, the Sin Eater began transforming the town's inhabitants into smiling, vacant shells of their former selves. Concerned, Roxanne set out to find Johnny Blaze, knowing that only Ghost Rider could help the town.

> ...THAT'S THE WAY, YOUNG MAN! LAY DOWN YOUR WEARY HEAD-- AND PUT YOUR FAITH IN ME!

> "...AND BELIEVE ME WHEN I SAY..."

Into the breach
When he arrived in Holly, Johnny quickly warmed to its friendly atmosphere. He found himself wanting to believe that the Sin Eater was actually doing some good. Attending church the following Sunday he accepted an invitation to come up to the altar. He lay down and prepared to have his sins devoured.

SIN CONSUMPTION
As the Sin Eater prayed over him, hideous tentacles reached out toward Johnny. However, they would find the Ghost Rider somewhat indigestible!

CENTURIOUS EMERGES

The attempt to devour Johnny's sins caused him to transform into the Ghost Rider. Finally, the real villain—Centurious—emerged. A battle commenced and Centurious proved victorious, capturing Johnny's soul inside the Soul Crystal.

THE SOUL CRYSTAL
While visiting ancient Egypt, Centurious obtained his mysterious Soul Crystal and began using it to capture the souls of others. He would then draw power from and consume them.

I NEVER NEEDED BLAZE!!!

I NEVER NEEDED HIM!

I... I NEED HIM.

Ghost Rider undone

At first Ghost Rider was pleased that Johnny Blaze's soul was captured by Centurious, but he soon found himself weakened by Johnny's absence. Attacking Centurious one last time, Ghost Rider managed to slice the Soul Crystal in two. The souls trapped inside escaped, but Centurious and Ghost Rider were sucked inside—leaving Johnny Blaze free at last.

THE ESCAPING SPIRITS SUCCESSFULLY RESIST.

THE SOUL-LESS MAN--IS NOT SO LUCKY!

NEW BEGINNINGS
For years the specter of Ghost Rider had lingered over Johnny and Roxanne. Finally they could start building a new life together.

CHAPTER 3

DAN KETCH

ALMOST A DECADE after Johnny Blaze finally doused his burning skull, another Ghost Rider rose to infamy. Hosted by naïve youth Dan Ketch, this Ghost Rider was not an itinerant wanderer like his predecessor. Instead, he restricted his travels to the streets of New York City, and was often seen stalking the cemeteries of Cypress Hills, Brooklyn. There, in the Super Hero capital of the cosmos, this new Ghost Rider battled every kind of evil— from petty street criminals to ancient supernatural forces. Armed with his Penance Stare and Hellfire Chain, he struck against armies of demons led by the appalling Lilith, Mother of Demons, and the legendary soul-less man, Centurious.

NOT ALONE
Dan Ketch was frequently accompanied by Johnny—now John—Blaze, as well as an enigmatic figure known only as, Caretaker.

DAN KETCH

THOUGH BORN INTO the Kale family, Dan Ketch had no memory of his birth mother, Naomi Blaze, née Kale. When still very young he and his sister, Barbara, were taken away to be raised by Francis Ketch. Although Francis's husband died not long after, Dan's childhood was largely happy. Francis was a devoted mother and Dan was close to his elder sister, who never failed to look out for him.

I STILL NEED TO COME TO MY *BIG SISTER* WITH MY PROBLEMS—

—AND THIS GHOST RIDER THING IS THE *BIGGEST* PROBLEM I'VE *EVER* COME ACROSS.

A WORLD GONE MAD

Dan always turned to his sister, Barbara, for advice. When she suffered near-fatal injuries, and Dan was transformed into the Ghost Rider, the comatose Barbara remained the only person he could talk to. Later, Dan was devastated when the psychopathic Blackout murdered Barbara in her bed.

Alas poor Ghost Rider
Dan's relationship with the Ghost Rider was always uneasy. Twice he tried to suppress Ghost Rider and twice they forged a truce, learning to fight as one to devastating effect.

DRIVEN TO DRINK
Following the death of her daughter, Francis Ketch found life ever-more difficult. Unable to turn to an increasingly distant and distracted Dan, she became lonely and depressed and drowned her sorrows in alcohol.

LOVE ON TRIAL

Growing up, Dan spent much of his childhood with a neighbor, Stacy Dolan. As they became older, they developed feelings for each other. A future together seemed likely until Ghost Rider arrived. Dan became increasingly unreliable, often disappearing without explanation, and their relationship soon started to feel the strain.

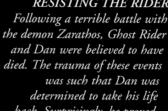

RESISTING THE RIDER
Following a terrible battle with the demon Zarathos, Ghost Rider and Dan were believed to have died. The trauma of these events was such that Dan was determined to take his life back. Surprisingly, he proved adept at suppressing Ghost Rider.

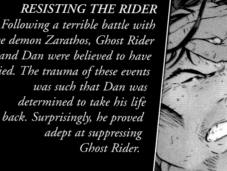

Dan gets a mentor
Not the brightest of Super Heroes on the block, Dan was poor at keeping his identity secret. Desperately needing to raise his game, Dan was hugely grateful when the previous Ghost Rider, Johnny Blaze, took him under his wing, even teaching him self-defense. Over time the pair became close and were unphased when they discovered they were actually long-lost brothers.

Family secrets
Watching her little boy grow up, Francis Ketch finally decided it was time to tell Dan the truth. Speaking to him one night, she told Dan that he was adopted—that she was not his real mother. Although he claimed this did not change anything, Dan was visibly shocked.

FAMILY REUNION
Eventually released from the Ghost Rider, Dan was then visited by a ghostly figure— Naomi Blaze. Asked to help lift the Ghost Rider curse from their family, Dan agreed, but the price was high...

NOBLE KALE

WHEREAS JOHN BLAZE'S GHOST RIDER was a reincarnation of Zarathos, the Ghost Rider borne by Dan Ketch had a very different history. When the Medallion of Power was broken, the pieces were divided between two families to be passed down through the generations. By the 1700s, one of these families was known as the Kales. It was headed by one Pastor Kale, the leader of a small town called Patience.

Wretched love

Pastor Kale was a hard man, but much loved by the townspeople. His good standing was threatened when his son, Noble, fell in love with a carnival girl, Magdalena. Fearing what the pastor would say they kept their love secret, until Magdalena became pregnant.

FOOL! YOU LIE DOWN WITH BEASTS! AS A BEAST YOU'LL BE PUNISHED!

LEAVE HIM BE!

A WARLOCK'S FURY

When he learned of Magdalena's pregnancy, Pastor Kale was furious. Magdalena knew that the pastor was in fact a warlock who struck bargains with the devil to guarantee the town's prosperity. While Noble was beaten viciously, Magdalena's punishment was much more harsh. Following the birth, their child was taken to be raised in "a good Christian home," while Magdalena was cursed as a witch and burned at the stake.

I CURSE YOU. I CURSE YOU ALL.

With fire raging about her, Magdalena cursed Pastor Kale and the townsfolk, calling on the demonic Furies to avenge her

A broken man

As she died, Magdalena was told that Noble was in the chapel, praying for forgiveness. In truth, his drugged and beaten body was hanging from the roof of a cellar, battered and broken.

Hell hath three furies

The demonic Furies dedicated their existence to avenging wronged women. Following Magdalena's death, all three Furies—the Maiden, the Crone, and the Dark Mother—fell upon the town to wreck havoc. Sworn to destroy every inhabitant, they set about their gruesome task. By day, they feasted on human flesh and at night they hunted, tormenting the town's inhabitants with a slow, terrifying death. Desperate, Pastor Kale turned to the demon Mephisto for help.

Cometh the day, cometh the Ghost Rider!

In return for Noble Kale's soul, Mephisto promised to arrange the Furies' destruction. Bones excavated from the town's graveyard formed the framework for a new warrior demon. Activating Noble's Medallion fragment, Pastor Kale ripped Noble's heart from his chest and placed it inside the skeleton. The first Ghost Rider had been born.

BATTLE WITH THE FURIES
Uniting Noble Kale's soul with the essence of a Spirit of Vengeance, the Ghost Rider was a formidable warrior. After three days of brutal fighting, the Furies were vanquished.

THEN IT IS AGREED THIS SOUL SHALL NOT BE CLAIMED BY EITHER REALM. IT SHALL BE FREED.

NO. NOT FREE. HE SHALL SERVE *BOTH* REALMS FOR *ETERNITY.*

WHAT?

The curse of the Ghost Rider

With the battle over, Mephisto returned to claim Noble Kale's soul, but before he could take his prize, an angelic entity, Uriel, intervened. The pair argued until a bargain was stuck. Noble Kale, in his Ghost Rider form, would live on through his descendents, with one person from each generation hosting his spirit. To ease his pain, Noble's memories were blocked, only his instinct to avenge the innocent would remain. The curse of the Ghost Rider had begun.

A NOBLE GHOST RIDER

IN THE CENTURIES since Noble Kale became the first Ghost Rider, the Ghost Rider curse has continued. In every generation, one of Noble's descendents has been forced to play host to his spirit, and become a Spirit of Vengeance. It is said that a Ghost Rider was glimpsed during the American Civil War, while it is almost certain that a Ghost Rider was seen in the trenches of World War I. While some embraced this fate, others, such as Naomi Blaze, resented the burden, and tried to escape it...

WHO DARES SPILL INNOCENT BLOOD?!

VENGEANCE WILL BE MINE!

CHNG

YOU DARE CALL HIM *SON* AFTER LEAVING HIM FLAT BEFORE HE COULD EVEN *WALK*?! HAH!

WELL, HE IS. I... I JUST WANTED TO TAKE A LOOK AT HIM. I HEARD ABOUT BARTON DYING AND--

Naomi Blaze: Ghost Rider

Naomi Kale married Barton Blaze and had three children—John, Barbara, and Dan. The Ghost Rider curse weighed heavily upon her, so, desperate to protect her children, Naomi made a bargain with Mephisto to save John, and had her younger children adopted. In the last days of her life, she went to see them all one final time.

DIDN'T I TELL YOU KIDS TO GET BACK TO WORK? COME ON.

BUT... WHO *WAS* THAT?

NOBODY WORTH WORRYING ABOUT.

WHO KNEW A TIRED EX-JUNKIE LIKE YOU COULD BE SO SLIPPERY? BUT YOU'RE NOT SLIPPERY ANYMORE, ARE YOU, DEAR?

BUT, YOUR MEDDLING DID WORK. YOUR *FIRST* KID'S BLOOD IS *CLEANSED* OF THE CURSE FOREVER. HE WON'T HAVE TO BE *THE* GHOST RIDER.

DYING BREATHS

After one final encounter with Mephisto's minions, a dying Naomi was visited by one of his servants. As she was carried to her grave, Naomi learned that she had failed—despite her efforts, John would still become a Ghost Rider.

Preparing the way

Following Naomi's death, Mephisto's servant prepared the way for the next Kale to bear the Ghost Rider curse. Before burying Naomi's motorcycle in Cypress Hills Cemetery, he branded its gas cap with the Medallion of Power.

DOESN'T MEAN HE CAN'T BE *A* GHOST RIDER.

MOTORCYCLE FOUND
Thirteen years after Naomi's death, her youngest son, Dan, found her bike in Cypress Hills Cemetery, in pristine condition.

I'M GOING TO MAKE THE BLEEDING STOP.

BUT THERE'S TOO MUCH BLOOD! SO HOT AND STICKY ON MY HANDS.

I'D DO ANYTHING TO SAVE HER.

GLITTER GAS CAPS!
Dan was attempting to save the life of his critically injured sister, Barbara, who had been attacked by the crimelord Deathwatch. As they took refuge in the cemetery, Dan found himself drawn to the motorcycle's glowing gas cap.

GHOST RIDER RETURNS

As he put his hand on the gas cap, Dan found himself transformed into the Spirit of Vengeance. The Ghost Rider curse had been passed from John to Barbara and, following her injury, finally to him. Although Naomi Blaze had been betrayed by Mephisto, he had underestimated her— Naomi's soul would not rest until she had accomplished her life's mission.

DAN, PLEASE DON'T DO THIS!

I HAVE TOLD YOU BEFORE...

...I AM NOT DAN.

...I AM GHOST RIDER.

DAN KETCH VS. THE GHOST RIDER
Like his mother before him, at times Dan Ketch resented Ghost Rider. On two occasions Dan tried to suppress it, to prevent Ghost Rider from taking over his body. Each time he eventually came to terms with Ol' Flamehead, even trying to find ways to provide assistance.

DAN KETCH'S POWERS

ALTHOUGH CALLED GHOST RIDER, Dan Ketch's powers were drawn from a very different source from those of his brother, John Blaze. Whereas John's body had been host to the demon Zarathos, Dan was a Spirit of Vengeance. Despite these differences their powers were broadly the same, but they manifested themselves in different ways. While John blasted others with hellfire, Dan wielded a hellfire chain and could sear the souls of miscreants with his Penance Stare.

Hellfire chain
Most often used as a whip, Ghost Rider's hellfire chain could also become rod-like, to be wielded like a sword or a baseball bat. On occasion, Ghost Rider even caused the chain's links to separate, and hurled them like a ninja's shuriken.

Agonizing transformation
As the years passed, Dan increased his control of the transformation into Ghost Rider. To begin with, he would change into the Spirit of Vengeance whenever an innocent life was threatened. Gradually, he learned how to cause the transformation and even how to prevent it.

PENANCE STARE
As a Spirit of Vengeance, Dan's Ghost Rider is set on punishing wrongdoers. With his Penance Stare he can force criminals to experience the pain they had caused others. Frequently, this would drive them insane. Only those without souls—men like Centurious—could withstand it.

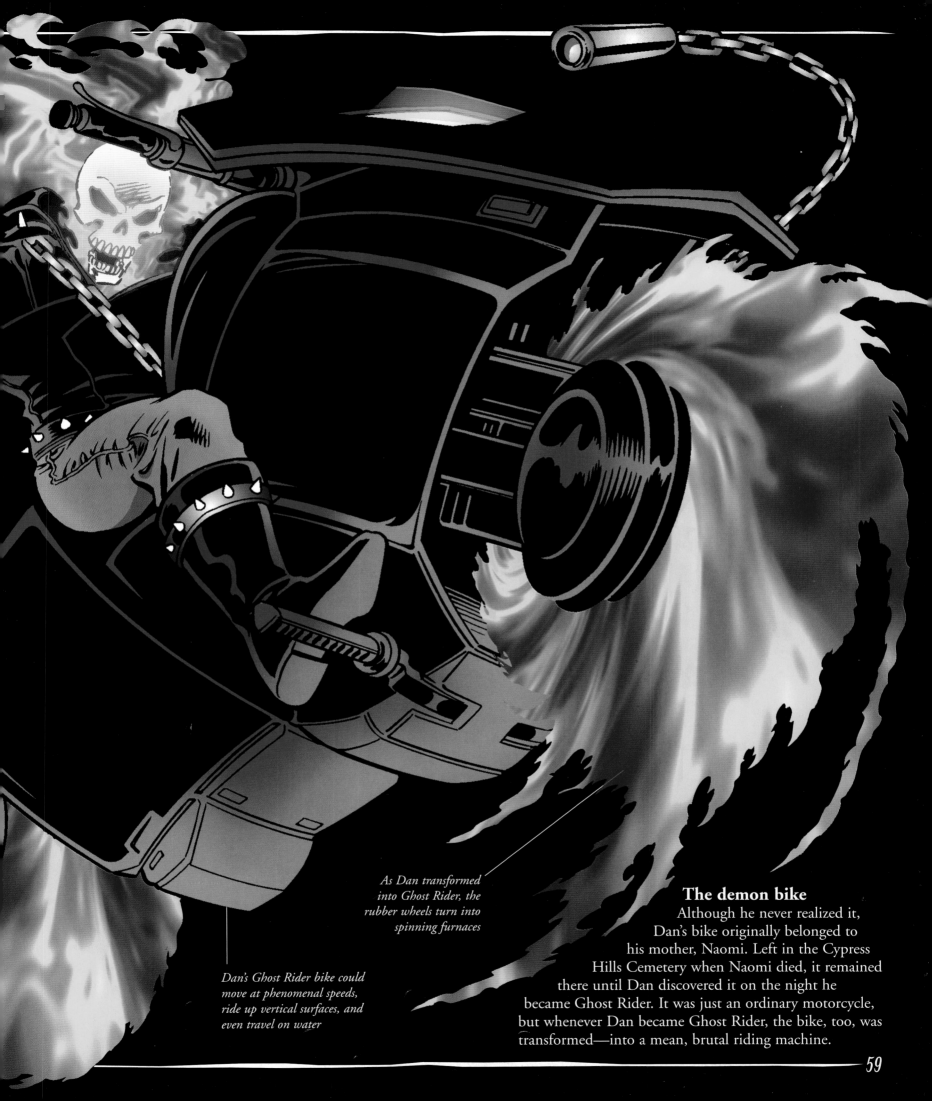

As Dan transformed
into Ghost Rider, the
rubber wheels turn into
spinning furnaces

Dan's Ghost Rider bike could
move at phenomenal speeds,
ride up vertical surfaces, and
even travel on water

The demon bike
Although he never realized it,
Dan's bike originally belonged to
his mother, Naomi. Left in the Cypress
Hills Cemetery when Naomi died, it remained
there until Dan discovered it on the night he
became Ghost Rider. It was just an ordinary motorcycle,
but whenever Dan became Ghost Rider, the bike, too, was
transformed—into a mean, brutal riding machine.

STACY DOLAN

EVEN AS A YOUNG child it was clear that Stacy Dolan was destined to have a challenging life. Her mother died when she was still young and her father was in the police force, so Stacy spent much of her childhood at the house of her mother's best friend, Francis Ketch. There she would play with Mrs Ketch's children, Barbara and Dan— friends who would have a huge impact on her adult life.

HUNTING GHOST RIDER
As a member of the Police Special Task Force, an elite police unit, Stacy was partly responsible for hunting down her lover's alter ego—the Ghost Rider—a task she performed with relish.

CHILDHOOD SWEETHEARTS
Growing up together, Stacy and Dan became increasingly intimate and as they approached adulthood their friendship developed into something deeper. In the years that followed, their love would be tested to the limit.

I'M SORRY, STACY, BUT WE'VE ALL BEEN THROUGH SO MUCH.

Pain of loss runs deep
The death of Dan's sister, Barbara, affected Stacy deeply. Years later, she would often make her way to Barbara's grave to talk through her troubles with her dead friend.

AND NOW THAT HE'S MOVED INTO THE CITY, I THINK IT MIGHT BE OVER BETWEEN--

FREEZE!

STACY?

BARBARA KETCH

DAD'S FOOTSTEPS
With her mother dead, perhaps it was inevitable that Stacy would follow in her father's footsteps and join the police force. Entering the police academy, Stacy graduated with flying colors. Like her colleagues, she was suspicious of the Ghost Rider and upon encountering him for the first time in a local cemetery she even attempted his arrest. Such was her eagerness as a young officer.

I STILL LOVE YOU AND...

...I'M NEVER GOING TO LET YOU GO.

NEVER.

Mourning Dan

At the climax of
the Midnight Sons' battle against Zarathos, Ghost Rider was forced to sacrifice his life. In that instant, Stacy realized Ghost Rider was actually Dan. Devastated, Stacy attempted to seize Ghost Rider's remains.

YOU WANTED YOUR ANSWER, SKI. YOU GOT IT.

I WANT IN.

I WANT IN ON BRINGING GHOST RIDER DOWN!

Code: Blue

Extremely able, Stacy rose
to prominence in the police
department and was invited to join
the Police Special Task Force, a unit
originally established to hunt down
Ghost Rider. Following her arrival, the
team had begun targeting Ol' Flamehead
again—and Stacy worked hard to help them.
When S.H.I.E.L.D., the secretive international
intelligence agency, eventually carried Ghost
Rider away, Stacy suddenly realized what she
had done. Still in love with Dan, she prayed
for his safe return.

A new love

Following Ghost Rider's mysterious
resurrection, Stacy's relationship
with Dan remained unsettled. With
the police ever-more antagonistic
toward Ghost Rider, the strains
between them both were beginning
to show. Lonely and spending more
time at work, Stacy began
romancing a fellow
officer, Lieutenant
"Ski" Sokolowski.

A FUTURE NEVER TO HAPPEN
*Shortly before his death, Dan Ketch
glimpsed a possible future in which he
and Stacy married and had a daughter.
Sadly, this future was never to be.*

FRANCIS KETCH

FOR FRANCIS KETCH, life was a series of brutal knocks, with a smattering of good fortune. Although blessed with a loving marriage, Francis and her husband were unable to have children. So, when an enigmatic stranger offered to arrange their adoption of a sister and brother, Barbara and Dan, the couple leapt at the chance. Sadly, when Francis's husband was killed by a robber, she was left to raise the children on her own.

> I'M SO SORRY, DANIEL. BUT THEY ARE GOING TO BRING BARBARA BACK TO US! REVEREND STYGE HAS PROMISED.
>
> PLEASE STAY HERE, DON'T INTERFERE, AND WE--BARBARA AND I--WILL *BOTH* BE HOME LATER.

Desperate housewife

Francis took the death of her daughter, Barbara, very badly. Her loss was made all the more difficult when Dan, her son, became increasingly withdrawn. Seeking solace in the local Stygian Church, she was taken in by its promise to resurrect Barbara. In truth, the Church wished to feed on Francis's soul.

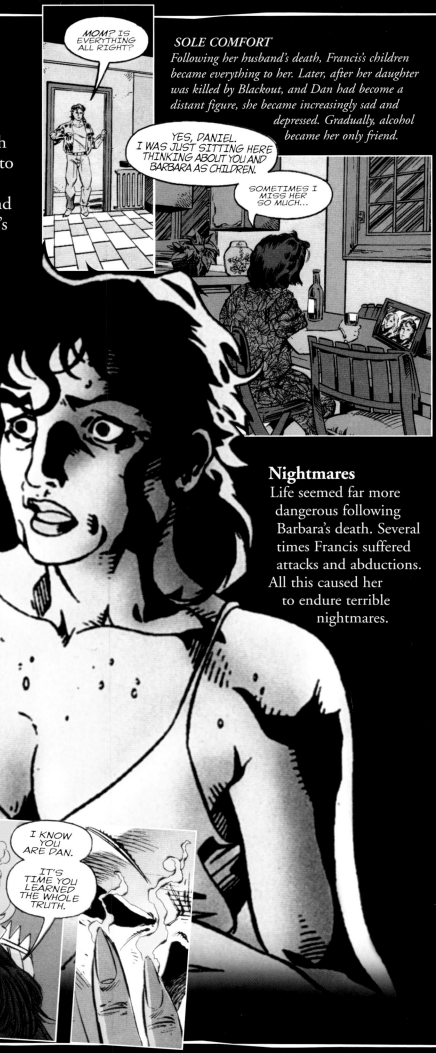

> MOM? IS EVERYTHING ALL RIGHT?

SOLE COMFORT
Following her husband's death, Francis's children became everything to her. Later, after her daughter was killed by Blackout, and Dan had become a distant figure, she became increasingly sad and depressed. Gradually, alcohol became her only friend.

> YES, DANIEL. I WAS JUST SITTING HERE THINKING ABOUT YOU AND BARBARA AS CHILDREN.
>
> SOMETIMES I MISS HER SO MUCH...

Nightmares
Life seemed far more dangerous following Barbara's death. Several times Francis suffered attacks and abductions. All this caused her to endure terrible nightmares.

TRUTH WILL OUT

Francis had denied it for a long time. She had even tried to forget that Dan and Barbara were adopted. But eventually, she was forced to admit the awful truth to herself, to admit that her beloved son, Dan, was the Ghost Rider. This did not make life any easier. Shortly after telling Ghost Rider that she knew who he was, Francis was kidnapped by the soulless man, Centurious. By admitting the truth, Francis had put her life in mortal danger.

> I KNOW WHO YOU ARE, GHOST RIDER.

> I KNOW YOU ARE DAN.
>
> IT'S TIME YOU LEARNED THE WHOLE TRUTH.

CAPTAIN DOLAN

ARTHUR GERARD DOLAN was a police officer of the old order—fair-minded, serious, and methodical. Over the years he had gained the respect of his colleagues, not only because of his ability to get results, but also because he had raised his daughter almost single-handedly following his wife's death. Inevitably, he didn't get on with everyone on the force, frequently clashing with the younger officers—men like Michael Badilino, who was constantly bending and breaking the rules.

ARE YOU SURE YOU'RE OK?

JUST A LITTE SHAKEN IS ALL.

NOW GO FIND THEM. YOU'VE WANTED *HIM* FOR SO LONG.

FATHER'S GIRL

Captain Dolan was hugely proud when his daughter, Stacy, chose to join the police force. He was full of admiration as she began making a name for herself and rose through the ranks. Nevertheless, these emotions were tinged with worry, particularly given her frequent encounters with Ghost Rider. Despite these concerns, he did his best not to cramp her style.

Deep Throat
Following his retirement, Dolan came to realize that ol' flamehead was actually a force for good. Frustrated that so many perpetrators of evil continued to evade justice, Dolan began working with Ghost Rider to bring them down. Sticking to the shadows, he called himself Deep Throat.

NO MORE FLOUNDERING AROUND... STRIKING OUT AT RANDOM.

I CAN HELP GIVE YOU A *DIRECTION*...

...BUT I *INSIST* ON MY PRIVACY.

In his spare time, Captain Dolan liked to keep abreast of the news

OH, POP... PLEASE DON'T DIE ON ME NOW. PLEASE.

A WEAK HEART
Shortly after learning that Ghost Rider was Dan Ketch, Captain Dolan discovered that Vengeance (Michael Badilino's alter ego) had gone berserk. Although injured in the effort to apprehend Vengeance, Dolan went on to make a full recovery.

NO. YOU WERE ALWAYS WAY TOO STRONG. YOU'RE NOT GOING ANYWHERE.

SNIFF! YOU BETTER NOT.

ALLIES

BASED IN NEW YORK, a Mecca for super heroes and villains of all persuasions, it was inevitable that Dan Ketch would come face-to-face with some of the most powerful individuals in the world. Over the years he would also fight alongside many of them against countless adversaries. Sometimes these partnerships were uneasy, but Dan found that sharing his difficulties with these super-powered friends could also be hugely rewarding.

Daredevil

After Dan helped Daredevil battle the evil Hand, Daredevil returned the favor and saved Dan in his confrontation with the spectral Succubus. A creature intent on absorbing the life energy of others, Succubus could also trigger Dan's transformation into Ghost Rider.

BATTLING THE BROOD
Following Blackout's near-fatal attack on Dan, Ghost Rider was unable to revert to his human host. Hunting for a solution, Ghost Rider became involved with Wolverine and the X-Men's battle against the Brood. Desperate to implant eggs in mutant bodies, these aliens threatened humanity.

SHARED EXPERIENCES

Dan's struggle with Ghost Rider was similar to that of other super-powered beings. Torn between wanting to work with Ghost Rider and suppress him altogether, a confused Dan had much in common with the X-Men member, Wolverine. Over the years, Wolverine had learned to control his bestial side. He warned Dan that locking up his demons would never work. They would always get out...

SHRIKER

Jack D'Auria was another of Dan Ketch's childhood friends. Yet Dan felt unable to share the secret of the Ghost Rider with Jack, concerned about its effects on their friendship. Little did Dan realize that Jack had already seen his transformation into Ghost Rider.

Mismatched heroes Ghost Rider and Spider-Man aided and abetted each other in their battle against the Hobgoblin

DR. STRANGE
When supernatural forces threatened to overwhelm them, Ghost Rider and Dan turned to Dr. Strange for assistance. Powerful and aloof, Strange nevertheless agreed to give what help he could, while also involving Dan in the Midnight Sons' battle against Lilith.

Caretaker's pawn
After vowing to keep Dan's secret, Jack was approached by Caretaker, who trained him to become the vigilante of the night, Shriker. In time, Caretaker hoped Shriker would provide support to Ghost Rider.

Allies against mephisto
After inviting them to the town of Christ's Crown, the demon Blackheart asked Dan Ketch, Wolverine, and Punisher to help him overthrow his father, Mephisto. Together they refused, preferring to use their powers to defend the citizens of that small township.

I'VE KNOWN YOU LONGER THAN ALMOST ANYONE.

JACK? JACK D'AURIA?

A friend in need
Dan and Shriker met when Ghost Rider was being hunted down by Code: Blue. Running out of places to go, Shriker offered refuge to his old friend and revealed his identity to Dan.

GHOST RIDER MEETS GHOST RIDER

FOR YEARS, JOHNNY BLAZE played host to the Ghost Rider, which jeopardized his relationship with Roxanne Simpson, and even his very life. Although he did some good during this time, many innocents also suffered. Learning that a new Ghost Rider was prowling the streets of New York, a dismayed Johnny—now calling himself John—set out to confront this new demonic entity.

YOU'RE JEOPARDIZING MORE INNOCENT LIVES. CALM DOWN.

GUNS SPEAK LOUDER...
Over time, John gradually learned to trust Ghost Rider. Lacking a way with words, John would not hesitate to put a gun to the biker's bony head if he thought Ghost Rider was going too far.

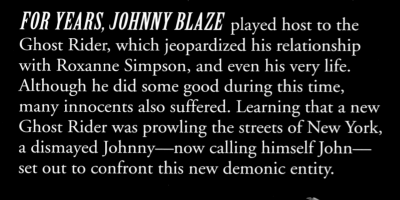

SO, DAN, JUST QUIT YOUR SQUIRMING AND THIS WILL GO A LOT EASIER ON BOTH OF US!

MMMPH... MMMOLLE MMMPPH!

I DON'T WANT TO HEAR IT ANYMORE, KID.

I KNOW YOU DON'T BELIEVE THAT IT'S ZARATHOS WHO POSSESSES YOU, AND I'M SURE THAT YOU BELIEVE THAT THE GHOST RIDER IS AN INSTRUMENT OF GOOD. BUT I KNOW BETTER.

TAKING NO PRISONERS

As he journeyed to New York, John Blaze assumed the worst—that Zarathos had returned. Understanding better than anyone the threat a resurrected Zarathos would pose to humankind, John was determined to destroy him once and for all. Tracking Ghost Rider until he changed back into Dan, John apprehended and bound the unsuspecting youth. It was hard for Dan to persuade John that his Ghost Rider was not Zarathos.

John was able to charge objects—his bike, knives, even guns—with hellfire

Although similar at first sight, there are subtle differences of appearance between Dan's Ghost Rider and John's

BROTHERS IN ARMS
After a struggle against Centurious, Lilith, and Zarathos, the Caretaker, who was a member of the powerful race called the Blood, finally told Dan and John the history of the Ghost Riders. With the battle won, he made one final revelation—that the pair were in fact brothers.

Testing relationship
Over the years, John's and Dan's relationship was tested to the limit. Following an attack by Hellgate, John's wife, Roxanne, was killed. Desperately upset, John warned Dan never to come near him again.

STAY AWAY FROM ME, DAN. IF I EVER SEE YOU OR THAT *THING* INSIDE OF YOU...

...I'LL KILL YOU BOTH.

ONLY IN HIS WORST NIGHTMARE DID *BLAZE* EVER IMAGINE THAT HE, ONCE POSSESSED BY THE DEMONIC ENTITY ZARATHOS WOULD BE RIDING SIDE BY SIDE WITH *GHOST RIDER.*

CARETAKER

A MEMBER OF that enigmatic and powerful race, the Blood, the man now known as Caretaker has walked the earth ever since his people battled against the demon Zarathos. Following that struggle, it was Caretaker who shattered the Medallion of Power and placed its fragments into the bloodlines of two families—the Kales and the Badilinos. As the millennia passed, Caretaker watched over these families, ready to intervene if danger threatened.

> I'M THE ONLY FRIEND YOU HAVE, BOY, SO YOU BETTER START LISTENING TO ME.

> THE NAME'S CARETAKER.

DAN GETS A FRIEND

Having arranged for Francis Ketch to adopt Dan and Barbara, Caretaker continued to keep a close eye on them, watching when Barbara was mortally injured and Dan became Ghost Rider. Still, he kept in the background, finally making himself known when he needed Ghost Rider to fight in a battle against the demon Lilith.

TRUST BREAKS DOWN
A cynical, manipulative individual with a violent temper, Caretaker was never able to win the trust of Dan Ketch or John Blaze. Thousands of years old, he was forever taking the long view and these luckless humans were simply pawns in his game.

68

68

MENTOR TO GHOST RIDER

He may not have won Dan Ketch's trust, but Caretaker's arrogance and brashness drove Dan and Ghost Rider to explore the vast power at their disposal. This enabled them to face down their future foes— Caretaker had provided a valuable lesson.

SEER

Since the battle with Zarathos millennia ago, the Blood had dispersed, no longer interested in what became of the Medallion of Power. Seer, a younger member of the Blood, was a rare exception. While Caretaker didn't hesitate to show his contempt for her, he was more than willing to accept Seer's help, provided she didn't attempt to undermine his authority.

Vengeance versus Caretaker

As Vengeance, Michael Badilino had been a servant of the demon Mephisto for a while, and, at his master's bidding, had attempted to destroy Caretaker. Although Caretaker was thought to have died in this battle, it wasn't long before he reappeared.

Caretaker weeps

Forming an alliance of nine supernatural warriors to form the Midnight Sons, Caretaker led the battle against Lilith and Centurious. It was in a climactic final battle against the demon Zarathos that Ghost Rider was forced to give his life. For a few moments, Caretaker's emotional barricades were broken and he experienced pain, regret... even guilt. Telling Dan's mother about her son's death, Caretaker apologized for the first time in his life.

When Seer began explaining the history of the Medallion of Power to Dan Ketch, Caretaker flew into a violent rage

DEATHWATCH

A RESPECTABLE FIGURE in New York society, the man some know as Deathwatch was also the chief executive of International Contractors Limited. Behind this facade, Deathwatch ran a sinister criminal operation, harboring ambitions to overthrow the Kingpin, New York's top crime lord. However, e0n this does not tell the whole story, for in truth Deathwatch was an extra-dimensional being, who fed on the pain and suffering of others.

A RESPECTABLE FACADE
By night, Deathwatch prowled New York in a mask; by day, he was just another businessman in a suit.

ATTACK ON NYC

To sate his appetite for suffering, Deathwatch absorbed the memories of his assassins, but he hungered for more. Obtaining three canisters filled with deadly toxins, he planned to decimate New York's population and feast on the resulting agonies. When the canisters were stolen by some youths, Deathwatch was forced to hire the mercenary Blackout to find them.

THE CYPRESS HILLS JOKERS
Confronting the youths in Cypress Hills Cemetery, Deathwatch demanded the final missing canister. Dan Ketch was shocked to see the youngsters being killed one by one.

Brutal tormentor
The youths couldn't remember where the last canister was—the cemetery was large and it had been hidden in a hurry. Furious at the damage they had done to his plan, Deathwatch would have killed them all if Kingpin's small army had not intervened.

Deathwatch's costume concealed his identity and allowed him to manage his criminal affairs without tarnishing his respectable persona.

STOP THEM!

BUDDA BUDDA BUDDA

Blackout in charge

Seeing that Deathwatch had been outwitted, Blackout seized the remaining canisters for himself. Before the toxins could be released Ghost Rider intervened and destroyed them.

BUT WHAT OF DEATHWATCH?

THE ENCOUNTER WITH *GHOST RIDER* DRAINED ALL HIS LIFE FORCE.

HE'S AS MUCH A HOLLOW HUSK AS THIS BUILDING.

WE'VE GOT TO TAKE HIM HOME.

ONLY THE *OTHERS* CAN HELP HIM.

EATHWATCH!

Deathwatch defeated

Although defeated by Kingpin, Deathwatch remained a force for evil. He transformed the basement of his corporate HQ into a seemingly benevolent homeless shelter, but in reality he planned to feed on their souls. Ghost Rider foiled this scheme. He overwhelmed Deathwatch's servants, Hag and Troll, destroyed the building, and killed Deathwatch.

DEATH NINJA

For a time Deathwatch also employed a small army of ninja warriors, in addition to his individual assassins—Blackout, Hag, and Troll. Despite being unable to kill a human, Ghost Rider drove one through with a sword, during a frenzied battle. When a ninja later returned from the dead Ghost Rider realized that he hadn't actually been human.

Death Ninja strikes

This creature, Death Ninja, had originally been hired by the soul-less man, Centurious, to infiltrate Deathwatch's organization. Now active once more, he wanted to take Ghost Rider to his master.

The dead will rise!

Although his body was little more than a desiccated corpse, Death Ninja was a formidable foe. However, a following a battle with both Ghost Rider and Suicide, he disappeared, never to return.

IT'S BEEN A WHILE, DANIEL BOY.

YOU DIED... WHEN I DIED. YOU WERE REBORN...

...AND NOW SO AM I.

THE BLOOD...

BLACKOUT

A CRAZED ALBINO PSYCHOPATH, Blackout was related to Lilith, the Mother of Demons, and possessed the ability to absorb light and throw whole areas into darkness. Having developed an insatiable thirst for blood, a dental surgeon gave Blackout a set of razor-sharp teeth with which he could slice into the flesh of others. With his new dentures and a rampant dislike of sunshine, Blackout had become a self-made vampire. An assassin-for-hire, Blackout's first encounter with Ghost Rider came while he was employed by Deathwatch.

ARRRRRGH!

A BEAUTIFUL HATRED BEGINS

When Blackout was hired by Deathwatch to track down a canister of deadly toxins stolen by a local gang of youths, he killed the culprits without mercy. After Deathwatch's defeat by Kingpin, Blackout tried to steal the toxins. Intercepted by Ghost Rider, a battle ensued which ended when Blackout tried to tear out Ghost Rider's throat. After being burned by hellfire, Blackout was left with a hideously injured face.

Blackout's revenge
Learning that Ghost Rider was in fact Dan Ketch, Blackout sought revenge. He went to the hospital where Dan's sister, Barbara, lay in a coma, and killed her. After that, Ghost Rider and Blackout became deadly enemies.

Psychotic slaughter

Deathwatch particularly enjoyed hiring Blackout to do his dirty work because of the great skill with which the psychopath murdered others. Able to scan Blackout's brain, Deathwatch reveled in the intense pain and suffering Blackout caused his victims. For some, killing was simply a necessary part of the job, but for Blackout it was an exquisite art.

Dan Ketch's death

For a time Blackout was imprisoned by the organization known as the Firm, itself a front for the malevolent activities of Centurious. In return for repairs to his face, Blackout was asked to capture Ghost Rider. He had no intention of complying. Instead he captured Dan Ketch and tore into his neck. Dan only survived by transforming into Ghost Rider.

Grudging truce

After battling Ghost Rider on and off for years, Blackout was eventually able to force his enemy to agree a grudging truce. Blackout promised not to pursue Dan or any of his family if Ghost Rider left him to go about his business. For a period this truce held, but it was only a matter of time before one of the pair tired of it. Although Blackout left Dan and his family alone, others were not so lucky, and Ghost Rider could not turn a blind eye to this for ever.

At the very top of the Empire State Building, Blackout felt the full glare of the sun

Burn Blackout burn

Sickened by Blackout's continuing activities, Ghost Rider finally lost patience. Chaining him to the top of the Empire State Building, Ghost Rider left Blackout to die under the rising sun.

LINDA WEI

Super Heroes are forever at the mercy of the press. Ghost Rider was always treated harshly and news reporter Linda Wei was partly responsible for this. She was paid by Deathwatch to tarnish Ghost Rider's image and she never missed an opportunity to misrepresent his activities.

No credibility

After the destruction of Deathwatch's headquarters, Wei blamed Ghost Rider. But as he began rescuing those trapped in the blast, Ghost Rider became a hero.

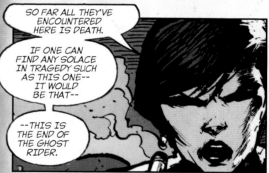

Doing penance

When Blackout began preying on her, Linda Wei finally tried to make amends for her behavior. Apologizing on air for her actions, she raised a gun to her head.

Before Linda Wei could kill herself, Blackout brutally murdered her.

VENGEANCE

MICHAEL BADILINO'S ADULT LIFE was forever marred by the tragedies he suffered as a child. During a confrontation with the John Blaze Ghost Rider, the soul of Badilino's father was seared by hellfire. Deeply traumatized by this, he committed suicide, killing his daughter at the same time. These events set the young Badilino on a path of vengeance against Ghost Rider. Nothing and no one would prevent him from taking down the demonic rider, once and for all.

THEN LET'S DO IT.

BADILINO VS. GHOST RIDER
A maverick lieutenant in the NYPD, Badilino was placed in charge of the new Police Special Task Force. His mission—to bring in the Ghost Rider.

MEPHISTO MEDDLES
When the Blood broke up the Medallion of Power, the pieces were divided between two families, to be passed down through each generation. These families were the Kales and the Badilinos. After his elder sister's death, Michael Badilino inherited both pieces of the Medallion, which drew the attention of Mephisto. Wanting to obtain the Medallion, Mephisto tricked Badilino into selling his soul in exchange for transforming him into Vengeance.

...YOUR SOUL!

Vengeance on duty
A Spirit of Vengeance like Ghost Rider, Badilino's powers included a Penance Stare. He agreed to serve Mephisto, but his hatred was too strong. Ignoring Mephisto's orders, Vengeance picked a fight with Ghost Rider instead.

THE MEDALLION THAT MEPHISTO SO DESPERATELY WANTS.

I'M GOING TO KEEP COMING BACK UNTIL YOU HAVE SUFFERED AND PAID IN FULL FOR ALL THAT YOU HAVE DONE TO ME!

Uneasy alliance
After Caretaker explained the truth about his origins, Vengeance realized that Mephisto was manipulating him. He formed an alliance with Ghost Rider and together they battled against Centurious, Lilith, and, finally, Zarathos.

SUICIDE

A lonely, self-pitying man, Chris Daniels didn't feel he had anything else to live for. His divorce had just been completed, his wife had taken their children, and he was unemployed. Desperate to end his suffering he put a gun to his head, but didn't have the nerve to pull the trigger. Doubled over with self-loathing, he cried that he just wanted the strength to kill himself.

Bad goes mad
When Badilino's police unit discovered a hoard of murder victims, his sanity snapped. Transforming into Vengeance, he went on the rampage. Thanks to Ghost Rider, Badilino eventually realized what was happening, but not before he had attacked Ghost Rider with a Penance Stare. To make amends he exploded his own body, killing crimelord Anton Hellgate in the process.

Beware the Prince of Liars
Mephisto offered Daniels the strength to kill himself, in return for his soul. It wasn't until later that Daniels discovered the catch—although he was now able to kill himself, he wouldn't actually die.

Enter Suicide
Calling himself Suicide, Daniels sought out Ghost Rider, believing that only the flamed one could kill him. After a series of confrontations the pair became uneasy allies. When Ghost Rider refused to kill the demon-host, Zodiak, Daniels did it for him.

Badilino in hell
Badilino's soul was sent to a hell dimension where it was attacked by scorpions. Dan Ketch eventually freed Badilino. In return Badililo transformed into Vengeance, helping Dan in his final battle against Blackheart. Badilino's current whereabouts are unknown.

SCARECROW

WHILE MANY OF Ghost Rider's enemies were born evil, some became corrupt over time. Scarecrow was born Ebenezer Loughton and suffered an abusive childhood, during which his alcoholic mother regularly beat him. Wracked with guilt, Scarecrow's mother alternated the beatings with gifts, leading him to associate rewards with bad deeds. This was the start of his psychopathic behavior.

SANITY SNAPS
At first he was little more than a petty criminal, but after a clash with Captain America, Scarecrow was placed in solitary confinement for a whole year and lost his sanity. Following his escape from an asylum he embarked on a bloody killing spree.

SCARECROW'S ARMY

Scarecrow's first encounter with Ghost Rider came shortly after his escape from the asylum. It ended with him being impaled on his own pitchfork. Reviving his body, the Firm enhanced Scarecrow's physiognomy, giving him superhuman strength and the ability to induce paralyzing fear in others. Using these abilities, Scarecrow began transforming his fellow test subjects into a loyal army.

AND WHY THE **SCARECROW** SHALL LEAD YOU ALL!

RELEASING FEAR
At large, Scarecrow felt insanely compelled to "release the fear" of everyone he met. He sliced open their bodies and stuffed them with straw.

Prisoner of the Firm

After an attack on the Firm by Ghost Rider, the police arrived to secure the scene. Finding a locked steel door, they began to cut through, unaware of what lay behind— Scarecrow and his army.

SCARECROW AT LARGE
Scarecrow and his army overwhelmed the police. More dangerous than ever, Scarecrow appeared all set to strike terror across New York.

DEFEATED
Scarecrow was apprehended by Ghost Rider and killed by Stacy Dolan.

AND THIS CANNOT BE ALLOWED.

KAROK

THE FORMIDABLE ZODIAK
Zodiak's powers were based on the 12 signs of the Zodiac: from Sagittarius, he had the ability to fire energy arrows; from Leo, lion claws; and from Taurus, bull's horns.

I HEAR YOU'VE BEEN LOOKING FOR ME, TIMMY! SOMETHING ABOUT A MESSAGE...

ZODIAK

NORMAN HARRISON was an ordinary man running a small New York bookstore that specialized in the occult. Then 12 demons arrived and asked to use his body as a host. Norman agreed and was transformed into Zodiak. When Zodiak embarked on a brutal killing spree he came to the attention of Ghost Rider. Unfortunately, Zodiak's numerous mechanical doppelgangers made it difficult for ol' Flamehead to exact vengeance.

EYE EYE
Zodiak wore a mask to hide the twelve eyes on his face— one for each of the demons that possessed him. Confused by this, Ghost Rider's Penance Stare would not work on Zodiak.

--IF ONLY TO STOP HIS *INCESSANT WHINING!* AND THIS HERE LITTLE BABY SHOULD DO THE TRICK ON *BOTH* OF YOU.

YOU'VE HEARD ME SPEAK OF MY MASTERS BEFORE. WELL, THEY GAVE ME THIS LITTLE BABY TO TAKE CARE OF YOU ONCE AND FOR ALL.

THEY TELL ME IT'S A GUARANTEED *DEMON-KILLER.*

AND YOU'RE THE DEMON!

DRUG BARON
To fund his masters' operations, Zodiak began running a drug-trafficking operation. Ghost Rider eventually tracked Zodiak down through his network of drug dealers. Zodiak had not been punished for the murder of an innocent child and Ghost Rider wanted to put a stop to the demon host's activities.

Zodiak defeated
During their final confrontation, Ghost Rider pursued Zodiak through New York's subways and sewers. Eventually Ghost Rider's ally, Suicide, threw Zodiak off a bridge and he fell to his death. To ensure he was gone, Ghost Rider and Suicide incinerated Zodiak's body.

LILITH

THOUSANDS OF YEARS AGO before the fall of Atlantis, Lilith was a malevolent force. A formidable sorceress, through unions with other demons she created a prodigious offspring—the Lilin. Known as the Mother of Demons, the greater Lilith's brood on earth became, the stronger she grew. Eventually she was defeated, and while many of her children escaped, Lilith was imprisoned in the dead body of a leviathan, located in the remote wilds of Northern Greenland. There she remained until the present day.

Lilith escapes

It was only when Arctic explorers happened across the leviathan that Lilith finally made her escape. Breaking through the creature's hide, she called to her children. She had waited a long time, but now Lilith was ready to wield power once more.

FAMILY REUNION
Gaining strength by feeding on the two explorers, Lilith's children also started to answer her call. Pilgrim, Blackout, and Creed were the first to be greeted.

WE WILL LOCATE OTHERS TO HELP US,

THOSE OF MY CHILDREN WHO HAVE NOT FORGOTTEN THAT WHICH I TAUGHT THEM SO LONG AGO.

SKINNER

Like many of Lilith's children, Skinner had abandoned all hope of his mother returning. Determined to lead a more settled existence, he married a human woman and had a child. Following Lilith's return, Skinner realized this life was at an end. Before embarking on his first mission, he returned home one last time— to kill his family, before Lilith could do it.

An unholy alliance

Sensing Lilith's return, Centurious forged an alliance with her, believing she could help him obtain the Medallion of Power. However, during a battle with Ghost Rider he suffered fearsome injuries. Zarathos had long been imprisoned in Centurious's body and, in his weakened state, Centurious could not prevent the demon from escaping.

With her hands alone, Lilith could inflict terrible injuries on her enemies

> CENTURIOUS!
>
> LILITH!
>
> STAND AWAY FROM BLAZE, OR--

> A BATTLE IS NOT NECESSARY.
>
> I PROPOSE A SIMPLE EXCHANGE. THE MEDALLION ON YOUR MOTORCYCLE...
>
> ...FOR THE KETCH WOMAN AND BLAZE.
>
> YOUR ANSWER?

> ZARATHOS, MY DEAR... ...LOST CHILD.

> COME, LET MOTHER HELP YOU.
>
> TOGETHER WE CAN FIND THE MEDALLION OF POWER.

> MOTHER...THE MEDALLION...?

Zarathos reborn

Following Zarathos's emergence, Lilith shifted her allegiance, announcing that the mighty demon was one of her lost children. Together she swore they would capture the Medallion of Power and begin a new rule over the earth.

A war lost

Utterly ruthless, Lilith and Zarathos were eventually confronted by the Midnight Sons. Overwhelmed by these forces, Lilith and her children were hurled through a rift and flung far away to another dimension.

> AFTER YOUR DEFEAT AT THE HANDS OF GHOST RIDER THERE IS NOTHING MORE YOU CAN OFFER ME. BUT ZARATHOS...

RETURN OF CENTURIOUS

Trapped inside the Soul Crystal, Centurious eventually escaped by binding Zarathos inside his body. Extremely weak, Centurious was forced to use others to consolidate his power. Through the Stygian Church, Centurious stole other's life force. After the Church's demise, he began developing a small but sophisticated army, under the cover of a reputable organization—the Firm.

The Medallion of Power

Centurious had his sights set firmly on the Medallion of Power. The fragments of the Medallion were embedded in the blood of his enemies—John Blaze, Dan Ketch, and Michael Badilino.

> ELSEWHERE...
>
> THE TIME FOR WAITING IS PAST.
>
> NOW IS THE THE TIME FOR CENTURIOUS TO ACT.
>
> MEMORIES... KNOWLEDGE... ONCE MORE.
>
> I NOW REMEMBER THOSE THINGS THAT I MUST CLAIM AS MY OWN.

Carnival of death

Even before his alliance with Lilith, Centurious's attacks on Blaze and Ghost Rider had become more direct. He killed many during his attacks on the Quentin Carnival, but still his objective was elusive.

MIDNIGHT SONS

IN THE DAYS before the fall of Atlantis, the first Midnight Sons came together to battle the dread demon Zarathos. This alliance between the Blood and the Spirits of Vengeance finally ended with the latter's destruction. Sensing the emergence of new demonic threats, Dr. Strange began forging the Midnight Sons anew. This coalition of nine unique individuals battled Lilith and the Lilin, together with the reborn Zarathos and his followers, the Fallen—members of the Blood who had turned their backs on their heritage.

MORBIUS

ZARATHOS

Victoria Montesi
While studying in Rome, Victoria Montesi was attacked by Lilith's forces. Protected by Sam Buchanan of Interpol and aided by Professor Louise Hastings, Victoria joined the Midnight Sons and began investigating the Darkhold, an arcane book of power.

FORCES WILL ASSEMBLED TO PREVENT ME FROM GATHERING MY CHILDREN!

BUT ALL THE SELF-PROCLAIMED HEROES WILL FALL BEFORE THE OFFSPRING OF LILITH!

JOHN BLAZE

Dr. Strange

Remaining in the background, Dr. Strange guided Ghost Rider and John Blaze to the Nightstalkers—Frank Drake, Hannibal King, and Blade. Although they distrusted Ghost Rider, the Nightstalkers, together with Morbius the Living Vampire, agreed to join the Midnight Sons. As the struggle with Lilith and her Lilin escalated into a war against Zarathos and the Fallen, Dr. Strange came to the fore. Transformed into the powerful Strange, he led them into their final battle.

STRANGE

I AM.. ...POWER!

MIGHTY STRUGGLE
The Midnight Sons were recreated to battle Lilith and Zarathos. Following Lilith's defeat, Zarathos united with treacherous members of the Blood, the Fallen. Defeating this dread axis of evil would take all the Midnight Sons' might.

HISTORY REPEATED
The first Midnight Sons defeated Zarathos through the sacrifice of the Spirits of Vengeance. This time, Ghost Rider paid the ultimate price—dying to destroy Zarathos once again.

SAM BUCHANAN

VICTORIA MONTESI

THE DWARF

PROFESSOR LOUISE HASTINGS

HANNIBAL KING

FRANK DRAKE

BLADE

CHAPTER 4

THE GHOST RIDER JOURNEYS ON

IN THE CLIMAX TO the Midnight Sons' battle against the demon Zarathos, Ghost Rider sacrificed both himself and his host, Dan Ketch. However, rumors of their deaths proved premature. Before long Ghost Rider and Dan were mysteriously reincarnated and were battling evil once again. Sadly, tragedy would continue to blight the lives of Dan Ketch and his brother, John Blaze. In the years that followed, both were to see their families threatened and experience the loss of loved ones. And worse was to come...

A NEW ADVENTURE
Great legends don't die, they are retold. The silver screen is the latest setting for John Blaze.

JOHN BLAZE AND THE QUENTIN CARNIVAL

THE YEARS FOLLOWING his escape from Ghost Rider were the happiest of John Blaze's life. Reunited with Roxanne, he bought the Quentin Carnival and started gathering a new family of carnival friends. At the same time, he and Roxanne began a family of their own—Craig and Emma were born shortly after their marriage. Although he was happy, deep down something still nagged at John, and following the appearance of a new Ghost Rider, his anxieties grew stronger.

AND WHAT BETTER WAY FOR YOU TO PAY FOR THE LOSS OF MY SISTER THAN WITH THE LOSS OF YOUR FAMILY...

...YOUR BELOVED CARNIVAL!

NO.

YES, BLAZE. THEY WILL ALL DIE BEFORE I ALLOW YOU TO JOIN THEM.

THEIR PAIN AND SUFFERING WILL ECHO IN YOUR EARS.

THEY WILL SUFFER GREATLY, AS MY SISTER HAS SUFFERED, BEFORE YOU ARE RELEASED THROUGH THEIR DEATHS.

...BACK!!

THEY'RE COMING FOR US ALL! KILLING IS STARTING!

REVENGE OF CENTURIOUS

In his days as Ghost Rider, John Blaze had battled Centurious a number of times and was partly responsible for trapping him inside the Soul Crystal. Having escaped from that prison and regained his power, Centurious was bent on avenging himself. So, as the members of the Quentin Carnival settled down for the winter, Centurious attacked.

IT'S TIME FOR THESE THINGS TO START PAYING...

...WITH THEIR LIVES!

The carnival fights back

Clara, the carnival's resident seer, warned the carnival folk about the impending attack, so they were ready to defend themselves. Although John was absent, rescuing one of the carnie children, his loyal friends had an arsenal of weapons and were ready to confront Centurious's demon hordes.

MY PEOPLE ARE BEING SLAUGHTERED DOWN THERE! WHAT HAVE I DONE TO THEM?

A BITTER BATTLE
By the time John finally arrived, the battle was raging fiercely. Although the carnival folk eventually proved victorious, the casualty list was high, and John's sense of guilt was heavy.

The army move in

Centurious's defeat wasn't the end of it. Before the dead could be buried, the army took control of the carnival ground. Angry at the army's presence and anxious to give his friends the respect they deserved, Blaze organized a secret trip to the carnival ground. While unable to retrieve the bodies, they turned the mortuary into a makeshift crematorium.

The army was securing the bodies of the dead carnies and demons. These would be used in weapons research.

AND I DON'T KNOW WHAT IT'S DOING TO YOU...OR TO US.

YOU'VE CHANGED, JOHN--NOT JUST YOUR APPEARANCE, BUT SOMETHING MORE.

EVER SINCE WE'VE COME BACK, YOU'VE KEPT ME AND THE CHILDREN AT A DISTANCE.

I'M JUST TRYING TO GET THINGS TOGETHER TO GIVE YOU ALL A GOOD LIFE.

Roxanne loses patience

With the carnival suffering from repeated attacks, Roxanne was becoming increasingly concerned by John's frequent absences. Worried about their marriage and children, Roxanne was keen for them to settle down.

TORTURED

Still hungry for revenge, Centurious finally managed to capture and torture John Blaze. He sliced aside John's skin to reveal the raging hellfire beneath. Following his rescue, John's friends managed to contain these flames by sheathing his body in a metal skin. In time, John's skin grew back, and he no longer needed the metal sheath.

STEEL WIND FOUND IT IN HER HEART TO FORGIVE.

I CAN'T.

BROOM!

THE END
Before rebuilding the carnival, John knew that he must first end his struggle with Centurious. So, he hunted him down, and fought and defeated him. Holding a shotgun to Centurious's head, John paused briefly. At last, their struggle would be at an end.

REGENT

LIKE CARETAKER, the man known as Regent belonged to the Blood and could wield enormous powers. In the millennia since their battle with the mighty Zarathos, the Blood had dispersed, and Regent had become increasingly envious of Caretaker. He was jealous of Caretaker's influence over those families who carried the Medallion of Power in their veins—the Kales and Badilinos—and he was frustrated that the Medallion's enormous power had been left untapped.

NO! I NURTURED MY POWERS ALL THE YEARS THAT HE WAS WASTING HIS CODDLING YOU THREE SPRITS OF VENGEANCE.

PREPARED
Since the Blood's dispersal, Regent had spent his days constructing a base in the Colorado Rockies and honing his abilities.

ROXANNE'S BARGAIN

Regent realized that if John Blaze ever had children, they would eventually inherit the Medallion of Power. When John was still the Ghost Rider and Roxanne was desperate to free him, Regent offered to provide assistance, in return for any children they might have. Years later, Roxanne gave birth to Craig and Emma, and as they neared adolescence, Regent prepared to make good on their agreement.

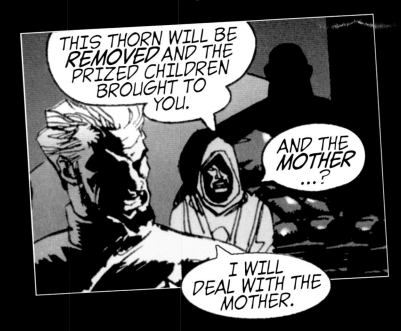

THIS THORN WILL BE REMOVED AND THE PRIZED CHILDREN BROUGHT TO YOU.

AND THE MOTHER ...?

I WILL DEAL WITH THE MOTHER.

A hidden army
Regent had also built himself an army, the assassin cult known as the Hidden. Indoctrinated through a ceremony of blood and pain, the Hidden were adept with swords, knives, and bows, and able to pass through society unnoticed.

THORN IN HIS SIDE
The only obstacles between Regent and Roxanne's children were John Blaze, the Blood known as Seer, and Roxanne herself.

A TRAITOR AMONGST FRIENDS

With the Quentin Carnival still under threat from frequent attacks by supernatural forces, John and Roxanne's children were sent away with brother and sister George and Marianne. Having known them for many years, John never thought he was actually placing his children in even greater danger. Indeed, even Marianne didn't realize the man she knew as her brother was in fact a member of the Hidden. When John finally realized the truth, George responded by stabbing him in the face, shooting Marianne, and carrying the children away.

John vs. Regent

Following their kidnapping, John Blaze managed to track down his children and Roxanne with the help of Seer, a young but powerful member of the Blood. Arriving at Regent's mountain base, John survived an initial clash with him. Then, making his way into the installation, he finally confronted Roxanne face-to-face. Gradually John came to understand the desperation that had driven her to make a deal with Regent in the first place, the torment she had suffered as the children grew up, and the worry his own repeated absences had caused. However, before they could escape they were forced to tackle Regent one more time. Getting out of the base was not going to be easy.

Regent destroyed

While Seer attacked Regent from behind and teleported the two children to safety, John and Roxanne were forced to flee on foot. The base had been set to self-destruct and they only had seconds to get away.

Family reunited

Returning to the carnival's refuge in Buck's County, Pennsylvania, John and Roxanne began working to rebuild their family. Little did they realize that yet more tragedy was just around the corner.

HELLGATE

AS ONE CRIMELORD PASSES AWAY, so another rises to take his place. After the demise of Deathwatch, Anton Hellgate masterminded his own ascendence within New York's criminal fraternity. Hellgate could fly and project deadly energy blasts from his hands, but he preferred to work through his servants. He might have remained unnoticed, except for a series of brutal attacks on New York police officers.

DEADLY ATTACK
Intrigued by the power wielded by Ghost Rider and Vengeance, Hellgate tried to capture one of them. He launched a vicious assault on John and Roxanne Blaze, and also on Dan Ketch.

Death of Roxanne

Hellgate's attack came while John and Roxanne were celebrating Dan Ketch's mysterious resurrection following his battle against Zarathos. Racing to safety with her children, Roxanne was struck by an energy blast. Although her remains were later discovered there was no sign of the children and John became convinced they were still alive.

TORTURED!

As well as killing Roxanne, Hellgate's attack led to the capture of Michael Badilino's alter ego, Vengeance. Intrigued by Vengeance's powers, Hellgate transported him to a laboratory. In a series of crude experiments, Hellgate forced Badilino to remain trapped, mid-transformation. With the help of Badilino's own notebook, Ghost Rider finally tracked him down to upstate New York, where he performed a daring rescue.

HELLGATE

Ghost Rider strikes back

Ghost Rider made his most telling strikes against Anton Hellgate during his partnership with the mysterious Deep Throat. Advised by Deep Throat to attack in a more methodical way, Ghost Rider struck against Hellgate's factories and warehouses, warning Hellgate that he would be next.

HELLGATE...

...I'M COMING FOR YOU!!

CHOAM

THE SCIENCE OF DEATH

Hellgate was a formidable opponent for Ghost Rider. He was no ordinary crimelord; as well as his own impressive physical abilities, he was also a master of thanatology—the science of death. Over the years, Hellgate had learned how to resurrect the dead and alter their bodies to give them superhuman powers. Dread, Rak, and Choam were just three of these super-powered zombies. Utterly loyal to Hellgate, they were part of a formidable army.

RAK

GO TO HELL
A mentally unhinged Michael Badilino followed Anton Hellgate to a conference in Atlanta City. Transforming into Vengeance, Badilino exploded his own body, destroying Hellgate and most of his servants.

DREAD

SNOWBLIND

Born blind and with no family to care for him, the man known as Snowblind grew up to be both self-reliant and ruthless. In part he survived by learning to project a "white field" that caused temporary blindness for others, but allowed him to see. Snowblind first came to Ghost Rider's attention during his investigation of a drugs ring.

Blind spot
During their first confrontation, Snowblind was unable to blind Ghost Rider. When Snowblind was hospitalized by Michael Badilino, Ghost Rider forced him to reveal Deathwatch's whereabouts.

Resurrected
Although he was killed for his betrayal of Deathwatch, Snowblind was resurrected by Anton Hellgate. His powers were augmented, and he became a far more serious threat to Ghost Rider. The only survivor of the explosion that killed Hellgate, Snowblind remains at large.

CODE: BLUE

ESTABLISHED BY MAVERICK COP Michael

Badilino, the Police Special Task Force was assigned the mission to bring in the Ghost Rider. In its early days, the unit was made up of seasoned officers who weren't afraid to break the rules when they needed to. Although their main target was the Ghost Rider, they also struck against the criminals that other police units were afraid to approach. Many frowned on their extreme methods, but the Task Force undeniably got results.

> COLONEL NICK FURY. I'M WITH S.H.I.E.L.D

> YOU GOT A MINUTE?

S.H.I.E.L.D. TRAINING

When Lieutenant "Ski" Sokolowski took control of the Task Force, it gained respectability. Ski was soon approached by Nick Fury of S.H.I.E.L.D., the international espionage organization. With the offer of S.H.I.E.L.D. training and equipment, the dream of capturing Ghost Rider became a possibility.

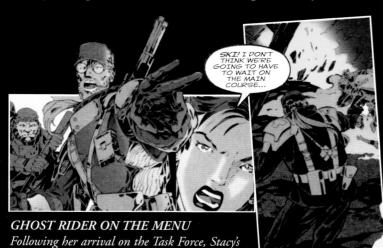

> SKI! I DON'T THINK WE'RE GOING TO HAVE TO WAIT ON THE MAIN COURSE...

GHOST RIDER ON THE MENU
Following her arrival on the Task Force, Stacy's first attempt to capture Ghost Rider came while he was battling the Next Wave mercenaries. With Wolverine's help he managed to evade the force.

FIREFIGHTING
Alongside the prestige that goes with being a crack police unit comes great danger. It wasn't unusual for the Task Force to be caught in serious gun fights.

Divided loyalties
A good police officer, hard working, and determined to get on, Stacy Dolan barely hesitated when she was invited to join Ski's Task Force. Increasingly resentful of Ghost Rider, the third person in her relationship with Dan, Stacy was eager to see him put away. So focused was she on this aim, Stacy could not see that, by hunting down Ghost Rider, she was betraying her oldest friend and many others she held dear.

Betrayed by S.H.I.E.L.D.
With the net closing in, Ghost Rider finally gave himself up. But, before he could be taken into custody, S.H.I.E.L.D. arrived and took control. Feeling betrayed, the Task Force could only watch as their prisoner was taken away.

> THEY USED US!

> USED US ALL TO DO THEIR DIRTY WORK!

JENNIFER KALE

MS. KALE.

OH, JEEZ!

DURING HER ADOLESCENCE, Jennifer Kale discovered she had inherited mystical powers from her grandfather. Years later, while living in New York, Dr. Strange approached Jen, asking her to help Dan Ketch. Ghost Rider had been attacked with a Penance Stare during a struggle with Vengeance. This had caused a series of magically suppressed memories to escape. For reasons he wouldn't explain, Strange believed that Jen was best placed to bring these memories under control.

AWAY FROM *THAT* ONE, RIDER. IT'S YOUR *WORST.* START AT THE *BEGINNING...SOMETHING EASIER...LESS PAINFUL.*

YES, AWAY...

YOU KNOW, THERE'S A NEW INVENTION OUT... IT'S CALLED A PHONE. THEY ALSO GOT ONE CALLED A DOORBELL.

TRY THEM SOMETIMES. THEY'RE ALL THE RAGE.

WHO WRITES YOUR MATERIAL...THE SAME GUY WHO CUTS YOUR HAIR?

I CANNOT SEE. THE SMOKE...

BREAKING AND ENTERING AND LAME INSULTS. VERY NICE, STEPHEN. CLASSY.

WE WOULD NOT BE HERE IF WE DID NOT NEED YOUR SERVICES, MS. KALE.

Reluctant aide
Boasting quick wits and a sharp tongue, Jen agreed to help. As she delved into Ghost Rider's mind she found that she needed all her powers to prevent his memories from overwhelming them both.

...NOBLE KALE.

THE SECOND FURY HAS ARRIVED!

PAST UNEARTHED
Digging deeper, Jen swept away the spells blocking Ghost Rider's memories, and unearthed the truth behind his origins. Under her guidance Ghost Rider learned that his original name was Noble Kale—a distant ancestor of Jen herself. He discovered that his wife, Magdalena, had been burned at the stake and that, as she died, she had called down the demonic Furies.

THE FURIES RETURN
The release of these memories caused the Furies to return. As they made their first tentative steps on this mortal plane, Jen prepared to fight them. The seemingly innocent request from Dr. Strange had landed Jen in a heap of trouble.

BLACKHEART

THE DEMON MEPHISTO had been a thorn in the side of John Blaze and Dan Ketch throughout their lives. A hugely powerful demon and the ruler of his own hell dimension, Mephisto was the envy of countless demon hordes. Boasting a vast arrogance born of hubris, Mephisto could not have imagined that his own son, the mighty Blackheart, would eventually be the one to bring him down.

> I WILL TAKE YOUR OFFERING AND *MORE!*

> BLOOD, MUSCLE, AND FLESH WILL BE MINE.

> I WILL LICK YOUR ASHEN REMAINS FROM YOUR CHARRED BONE!

> NOOOOOO OOO!

INVOKED
Blackheart's path to power began when worshippers in the town of Christ's Crown invoked his presence.

HEARTS OF DARKNESS

Arriving on the mortal plane, Blackheart showed no gratitude and consumed his devoted worshippers. Not lacking in ambition or gall, he invited Punisher, Wolverine, and Ghost Rider to ally with him in his effort to destroy Mephisto. They all refused, recognizing that Blackheart was as treacherous as his father.

Making enemies
Thus rejected, Blackheart tried to blackmail Punisher, Wolverine, and Ghost Rider. Placing the entire town in a trance, he abducted a young girl, Lucy Crumm. His actions only stirred the trio's enmity. Following a full-on attack, Blackheart was driven off.

> FIGHT!

> NOW ALL YOU'VE DONE IS MAKE US MAD BLACKIE!

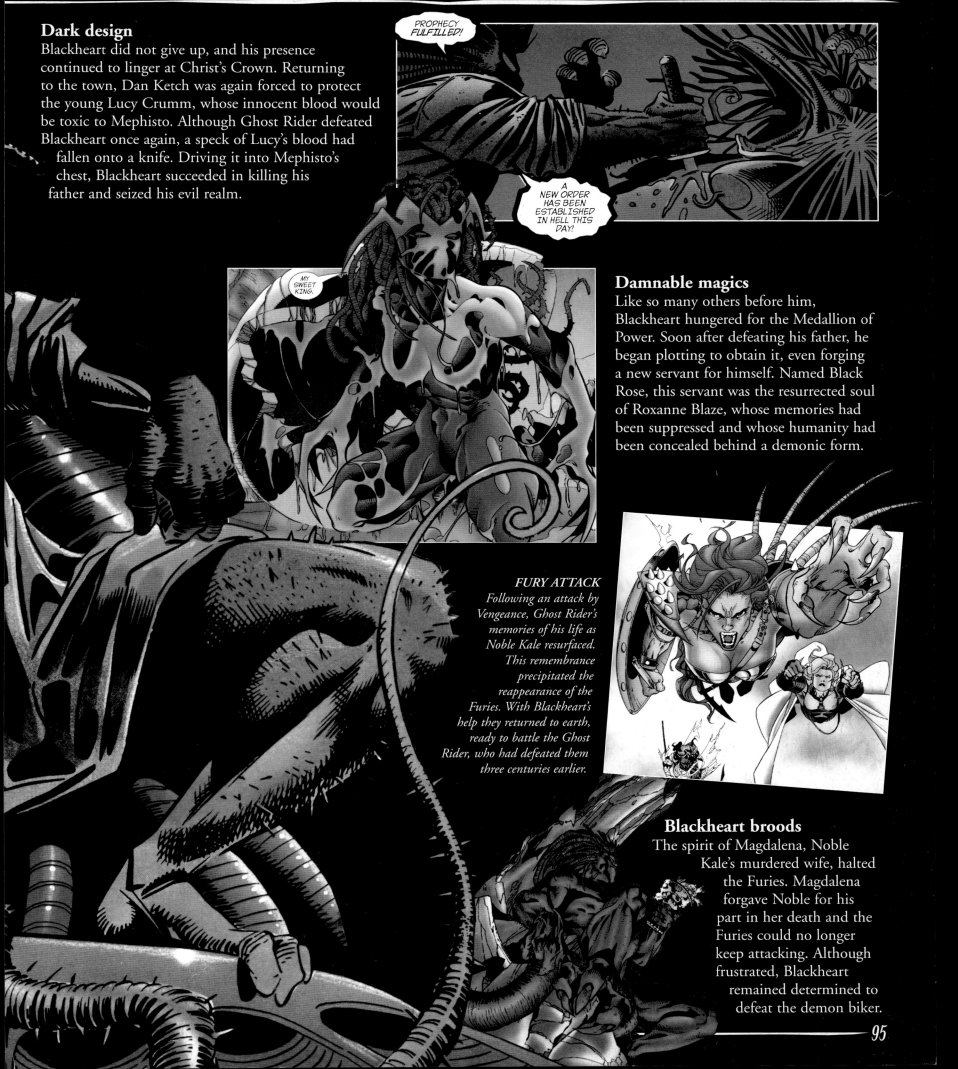

Dark design

Blackheart did not give up, and his presence continued to linger at Christ's Crown. Returning to the town, Dan Ketch was again forced to protect the young Lucy Crumm, whose innocent blood would be toxic to Mephisto. Although Ghost Rider defeated Blackheart once again, a speck of Lucy's blood had fallen onto a knife. Driving it into Mephisto's chest, Blackheart succeeded in killing his father and seized his evil realm.

PROPHECY FULFILLED!

A NEW ORDER HAS BEEN ESTABLISHED IN HELL THIS DAY!

MY SWEET KING.

Damnable magics

Like so many others before him, Blackheart hungered for the Medallion of Power. Soon after defeating his father, he began plotting to obtain it, even forging a new servant for himself. Named Black Rose, this servant was the resurrected soul of Roxanne Blaze, whose memories had been suppressed and whose humanity had been concealed behind a demonic form.

FURY ATTACK
Following an attack by Vengeance, Ghost Rider's memories of his life as Noble Kale resurfaced. This remembrance precipitated the reappearance of the Furies. With Blackheart's help they returned to earth, ready to battle the Ghost Rider, who had defeated them three centuries earlier.

Blackheart broods

The spirit of Magdalena, Noble Kale's murdered wife, halted the Furies. Magdalena forgave Noble for his part in her death and the Furies could no longer keep attacking. Although frustrated, Blackheart remained determined to defeat the demon biker.

A GHOST RIDER NO MORE?

HAVING OVERTHROWN MEPHISTO, Blackheart wished to extend his realm. The only obstacle in his way was Ghost Rider—if he could capture Ghost Rider's soul and obtain the Medallion of Power, Blackheart would be powerful beyond compare. Blackheart had attempted this before, striking against Ghost Rider with force. This time he was determined to be subtle, and defeat his enemy with guile and cunning.

PAO FU
After escaping from her minder, illegal immigrant Pao Fu was tracked down and killed. Resurrected by Blackheart, she became a Spirit of Vengeance.

Spirits of Vengeance

Blackheart began creating new Spirits of Vengeance. With the assistance of his servant Black Rose, he invited the demons Wallow and Verminus Rex—both recently defeated by Ghost Rider—to ally with him. In the mortal realm he resurrected a recently murdered illegal immigrant and transformed her into the demon Pao Fu. Finally, he bound together the souls of a dog and his master to create Doghead.

Black Rose
Wallow
Pao Fu
Verminus Rex
Doghead

I HAVE CREATED NEW SPIRITS OF VENGEANCE, AS IT IS MY RIGHT.....AND THEY WILL *SUBJUGATE* THE NEW WORLD IN *MY NAME.*

WHAT OF THE *GHOST RIDER?* IS HE NOT THE TRUE SPIRIT OF *VENGEANCE?* WILL HE NOT BE A *THORN* TO YOUR *PLANS?*

INTO THE VOID
Having assembled his Spirits of Vengeance, Blackheart and Black Rose traveled into another hell dimension to retrieve the preserved body of Noble Kale.

A TEMPTING OFFER

Meeting with Ghost Rider, Blackheart invited him to lead his new Spirits of Vengeance. At first Ghost Rider refused, but gradually he was tempted. In return he would be given back his original body, that of Noble Kale, and would no longer have to share another's body. In addition, the Ghost Rider curse would be lifted from the Kale family.

YOU CAN HAVE YOUR BODY *BACK.* YOU CAN FREE YOUR FAMILY *FROM YOUR CURSE.*

YOU CAN *EVEN HAVE LOVE.*

AGREE TO LEAD THE NEW SPIRITS OF VENGEANCE. *TEACH* THEM TO DO THE JOB YOU HAVE DONE FOR THE PAST *TWO HUNDRED YEARS...*

...AND YOU CAN HAVE IT *ALL.*

OH MY, THIS IS SO *WRONG.*

ROXANNE RESURRECTED

As he bargained with Blackheart, Ghost Rider realized that Blackheart's servant, Black Rose, was in fact John Blaze's wife—Roxanne. When Blackheart suggested they seal their agreement with Ghost Rider's marriage to Pao Fu, Ghost Rider demanded that he marry Black Rose as well. The agreement made, Ghost Rider's heart was placed in the body of Noble Kale.

WHAT IS IT, RIDER? YES OR NO?

YES OR NO?

YOUR *FAMILY* IS FREED FROM YOUR CURSE. YOUR *MISSION* IS NOW YOURS AND *YOURS ALONE*.

AND ALL YOU HAD TO DO WAS *MAKE A DEAL* WITH *LORD BLACKHEART*.

STILL SUSPICIOUS
Ghost Rider had been given back his own flesh and blood body and the curse had been lifted from the Kale family, yet still he sensed that there was treachery and betrayal on Blackheart's mind.

REBORN
For over two centuries, Ghost Rider has been separated from his original human body. Finally he was complete.

NO. THERE IS ONE MORE THING. ONE GIFT OF IDENTITY THAT I WILL NOT REALIZE UNTIL THE VOID ENDS... SOMETHING HIDDEN DEEP INSIDE OF ME UNTIL I MAKE THE CHOICE TO USE IT.

FOR I AM THE SECRET FIRE...THE FLAME THAT ENDS THE WORLD. THE LAST JUDGE AND EXECUTIONER... ...FOR I AM THE ANGEL OF DEATH.

ALIEK!

RIDE IT OUT, DANNY. RIDE IT OUT.

THE GHOST RIDER'S MEMORIES ARE INTERFERING WITH YOUR *OWN* BRAIN PATTERNS.

GCK..... GK.. GCK...

Dan rides to the rescue
While Blackheart schemed, Dan Ketch was looking for a way to help Ghost Rider. Guided by the ghost of his mother, Naomi, Dan delved into Ghost Rider's memories. There he unearthed a secret that could destroy Blackheart.

ULTIMATE SACRIFICE
By unearthing his dead mother's bones, Dan was transported to Blackheart's realm, where battle was raging. Danny gave Ghost Rider the knowledge to defeat the demon, but although Ghost Rider succeeded in destroying Blackheart, Dan also died.

ICEBOX BOB

FOLLOWING THE DESTRUCTION of Centurious, John Blaze dedicated himself to rebuilding the Quentin Carnival, although never once forgetting that his children were still missing. John's old carnie friends had remained loyal to him and soon they were touring the country once again. While working on his bike one morning, John was approached by an enigmatic young boy, Holden Blevins, and asked to help battle Icebox Bob, a local bogeyman. A murderer who killed his victims with an ice pick, Icebox Bob had been executed years earlier. However, his spirit lived on in a hell dimension, and from there he returned to torment others.

THAT'S HIM! I SAW HIM AT SCHENKER'S STORE IN TOWN! IT WAS A MUMMIFIED HUMAN BODY--

STUFFED!
Passing through a small town, members of the Quentin Carnival saw Icebox Bob's stuffed body on display in a local store.

BE SURE TO COME BACK NEXT MONTH FOR ANOTHER COLD BLAST FROM ICEBOX BOB!

I'LL BE WAITING...

Vengeance
Taunted by Icebox Bob, who claimed to know where his children were, John and Holden traveled to his world. Despite pounding him with hellfire, the undead psychopath refused to die. It was only when Holden stabbed him with a steel nail file, engraved with the powerful number 7, that the creature was finally defeated.

> EMMA! CRAIG!

> REACH OUT FOR ME!

BLAZE'S CHILDREN

JUST AS NAOMI BLAZE had failed to protect her children from the Ghost Rider curse, John Blaze also failed to protect his offspring. Although Craig and Emma's early years were peaceful, it became more difficult to keep them safe following Ghost Rider's return. Ultimately the siblings disappeared altogether, just seconds after their mother's death.

> YOU CAN'T HAVE THEM *BACK,* BLAZE--

> --NOT JUST *YET!!*

> DADDYYYYY!!

Rescue foiled
During his final struggle with Icebox Bob, John glimpsed his children at a window. Although he tore his way toward them, he was too late—Baal, a demonic entity, seized them and carried them away.

THE WENDIGO
A Native American spirit being, the Wendigo padded across dimensions, seemingly unaware of its surroundings. As it passed through their cell, Craig, Emma, and their friend Jesse leapt onto its back and were carried away.

BATTLING BAAL
Icebox Bob was not responsible for kidnapping John Blaze's children; in truth he was little more than bait. By crossing into Icebox Bob's world, Blaze had weakened the dimensional barriers preventing the escape of his true enemy—the demon Baal. Following Blaze's arrival, and Craig and Emma's escape on the back of the Wendigo, these barriers finally collapsed. At last, Baal was free to inflict his wrath on other worlds.

> IT'S THE *WENDIGO!!*

> LOOK, JESSIE HE'S GOT THE *NAIL FILE* YOU PULLED OUTTA *ICEBOX BOB'S* HEAD!

> IF *HE* CAN GO RIGHT THROUGH THESE *WALLS...*

> MAYBE WE CAN HITCH A *RIDE* WITH HIM!

> WHERE ARE WE GOING?

> WHO *CARES,* AS LONG AS IT'S OUTTA *HERE!*

FIGHTING ON
Although they could have returned to their father, Craig and Emma chose to remain with Wendigo and assist him in his pursuit of Baal so that others wouldn't suffer as they had done.

GHOST RIDER RETURNS

WITH HIS BROTHER, Dan, dead and with no hope of finding his children, John Blaze decided to put his old life behind him. For three years he worked as an accountant, riding nothing more exciting than the subway, and sitting behind a littered desk. Living with his grumbling girlfriend, Chloe, John tried to forget his previous existence, but he couldn't help feeling bored, frustrated, and deeply unhappy. Somewhere in the back of his mind, John's old wanderlust was crying out to be heard.

...CHLOE, LISTEN, I CAN'T GET *INTO* THIS RIGHT NOW. BABY, I'M AT *WORK*...

I DON'T REMEMBER SEEING *STUNT RIDER* ON YOUR RESUME...

The truth will out
When he joined his accountancy firm, John somehow managed to keep his stunt-riding past a secret. However, he had been so famous, it was inevitable that one day someone would uncover the truth.

A FAMILIAR ITCH
One day John left his office and wandered down to the garage. As he passed a Harley Davison, he began to experience a familiar burning sensation...

GHOST RIDER AGAIN
Transforming into Ghost Rider for the first time in two decades, John discovered that ol' Flamehead had changed. As well as being more difficult to control, John's demon was now far more violent—in its quest for vengeance, a bloody trail of death was strewn in its wake.

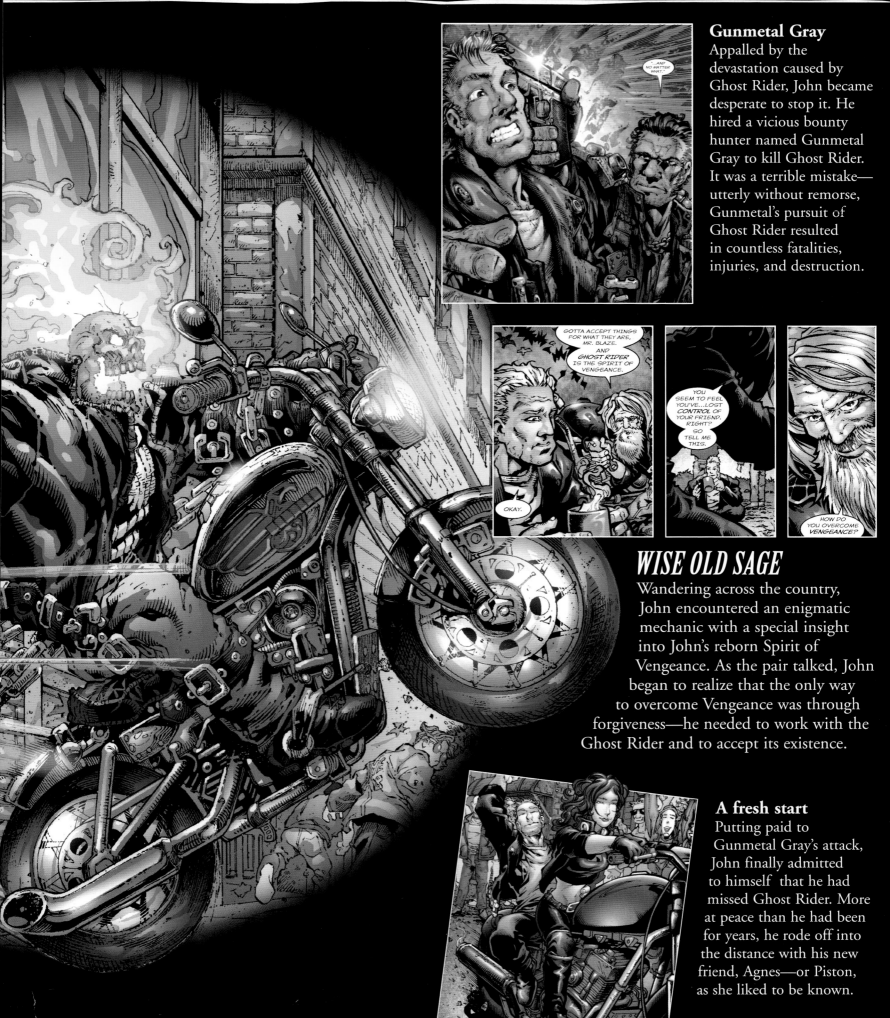

Gunmetal Gray
Appalled by the devastation caused by Ghost Rider, John became desperate to stop it. He hired a vicious bounty hunter named Gunmetal Gray to kill Ghost Rider. It was a terrible mistake—utterly without remorse, Gunmetal's pursuit of Ghost Rider resulted in countless fatalities, injuries, and destruction.

WISE OLD SAGE
Wandering across the country, John encountered an enigmatic mechanic with a special insight into John's reborn Spirit of Vengeance. As the pair talked, John began to realize that the only way to overcome Vengeance was through forgiveness—he needed to work with the Ghost Rider and to accept its existence.

A fresh start
Putting paid to Gunmetal Gray's attack, John finally admitted to himself that he had missed Ghost Rider. More at peace than he had been for years, he rode off into the distance with his new friend, Agnes—or Piston, as she liked to be known.

ROAD TO DAMNATION

THE GHOST RIDER had harried John Blaze for almost 30 years, and it was inevitable that his original pact with Mephisto would one day catch up with him. When demons finally arrived to drag the Ghost Rider down to the pits of hell, he rode like a lunatic, but it was to no avail and eventually they wore him down. Languishing in Hades, each day he would ride on his flaming bike, demonic hordes snapping at his heels as he raced for the gates of hell. Each day the gates would close, just as he reached them, and the demons would fall upon him.

Earl Gustav

Kazann's escape from hell was enabled by Earl Gustav, a ruthless quadriplegic billionaire with sociopathic tendencies. Securing Kazann's escape was hugely complicated, with one demand followed by another, more challenging one. Requiring a blood sacrifice to open the portal through to hell, Gustav sacrificed his entire board of directors.

> MY LORD...I HAVE DONE ALL THAT YOU WANTED OF ME...BUT...

> BUT, AT EVERY STAGE IN OUR TRANSACTION, YOU ALWAYS SEEM TO HAVE ONE MORE DEMAND...

CELESTIAL WAR

John suffered his hellbound torment for two years, but hope came at last when the demon Kazann escaped from the pit to threaten the corporeal world. For countless millennia, Kazann and the angel Malachi had exchanged sensitive information to increase their standing in their respective realms. Kazann's escape threatened to expose this treachery and Malachi needed to get him back, fast.

> RECKON YOU'RE WISHIN' YOU STAYED HOME WITH YOU'RE MOMMA TONIGHT, BOY.

> MMMMMMFF?

> AN' SPEAKIN' O' CHANGES: YOU'RE NEW NAME IS BUTTVIEW.

Hoss and Buttview

One of hell's most reliable tracker scouts, Hoss used the most brutal techniques to find Kazann. He remodeled the body of a rogue biker to serve as his guide and named him Buttview.

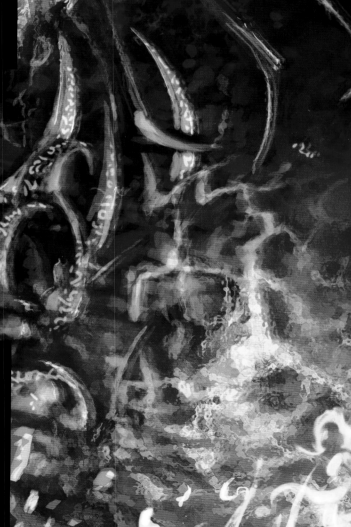

BARGAINING WITH AN ANGEL

In return for capturing Kazann, Malachi offered Ghost Rider the prospect of permanent escape from hell. Ghost Rider had no choice but to accept. However, his search for Kazann did not go smoothly. After losing his bike to the archangel Ruth, he was then forced to forge an unlikely partnership with the merciless Hoss.

ARCHANGEL
RUTH
Ghost Rider's first encounter with the archangel Ruth, who was also searching for Kazann, ended badly when she seized his bike.

Betrayed
Wrenching Kazann back to hell, Ghost Rider realized he had been betrayed. While Malachi was destroyed for his treasonous behavior, Blaze was returned to hell.

Even pushing his flame-bike to the very limit, Ghost Rider was unable to escape the demons surging at his back.

GHOST RIDER 2099

IN ONE POSSIBLE FUTURE, a very different Ghost Rider was to emerge. Kenshiro "Zero" Cochrane belonged to the Hotwire Martyrs, a group of data pirates. However, when he obtained some sensitive information, a corrupt multinational corporation, D/Monix, ordered him dead. But death was merely physical—with Zero's mind uploaded into cyberspace, an enigmatic artificial intelligence named Ghost-Works offered him new life as a Warbot, a cybernetic warrior.

The Warbot's skull-like head resembled that of the original Ghost Rider

AND YOU SOLD ME **OUT!**

I **DID** WHAT **ANY** LAW-ABIDING CORPORATE EMPLOYEE WOULD'VE DONE.

I HAD A DUTY TO SOCIETY.

BETRAYED BY HIS OWN FATHER

Infiltrating D/Monix's headquarters, Zero confronted his father, Harrison Cochrane, an executive in the corporation. The pair had long ago fallen out as Harrison was angry at his son's anarchic behavior. Even so, Zero was shocked to discover that it was his father who had ordered his death.

GHOST-WORKS
Following the death of his physical body, Zero was presented to the Ghost-Works. Accustomed to navigating through cyberspace, Zero's sense that he was trapped inside a surrealist painting did not overwhelm him.

YOU'VE TRAVELED TO A DIMENSION OF NEITHER SHADOW NOR SUBSTANCE.

SUBMITTED FOR YOUR APPROVAL, KENSHIRO COCHRANE--

A REFUGE HIDDEN AMONG THE INTERSTITIAL REGIONS OF CYBER-SPACE, UNKNOWN TO MAN.

HERE DWELL A CLASS OF INTELLECTS MORE MATHEMATICAL THAN MATERIAL; ARTI-FICIAL INTELLIGENCES FREED OF HUMAN BONDAGE.

MEMORY TRICKS
Zero gradually realized that the Ghost-Works were not as benevolent as they had first appeared. To better control him, they had altered and suppressed some of his memories. When he attempted to access these his body started malfunctioning.

SOUNDS TO ME LIKE YOU'VE BEEN TAMPERED WITH.

WHOEVER MADE YOU... WHATEVER IT IS YOU ARE NOW, MAYBE?

I'LL TAKE THAT AS A "YES."

CYBERNETIC WARRIOR

A sophisticated cybernetic soldier, Zero's Warbot body resembled the Ghost Rider's of the previous century, the memory of which continued to haunt society. Cloaked in silicon, the Warbot boasted carbon-steel fiber optics and super-dense metatasking nano-processors. Just as the original Ghost Rider was able to sear souls with its Penance Stare, so the Warbot's laser eyes could scorch the flesh of its enemies. There was just one problem—the Warbot constantly needed recharging.

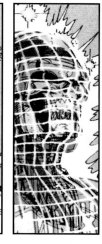

Stealth field

A solidogram camouflage system meant that the Warbot could mimic Zero's body and pass as human. In fact, after undertaking detailed scans, Ghost Rider could copy just about anybody. In his human form, Zero became reacquainted with his old friends, although when they realized what he now was, many were wary.

Those we leave behind

Before the demise of his physical body, Zero had a tumultuous relationship with his girlfriend, Kylie. However, after his disappearance Kylie worked hard to find him, employing cyber-cowboy Jimmy Alhazared to help her.

Ghost Rider's left hand was made from a morphable nanomer alloy, enabling it to change size and shape, and perform diverse functions

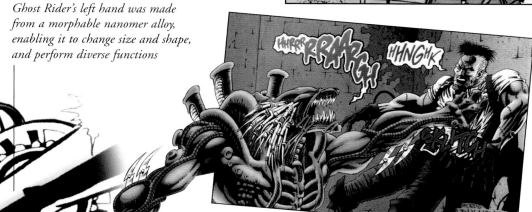
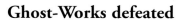

A SPIRIT OF VENGEANCE
Traveling the streets of Transverse City, Ghost Rider encountered a number of cybernetic killing machines. Controlled by a group of wealthy children, they were being used to murder vagrants for sport.

Ghost-Works defeated

Later, Zero discovered that he was just a copy of himself, and that Ghost-Works had edited his personality to control him. When the original Zero escaped from his prison in cyberspace, he took revenge. To stop Ghost-Works's manipulation of humanity, Zero compromised their self-determination programming. Once more, humanity was free to determine its own future.

GHOST RIDER: THE MOVIE

SEVENTEEN-YEAR-OLD JOHNNY BLAZE CO-STARS, with his father, Barton, in the *Amazing Blazing Stunt Cycle Spectacular.* A spirited youth, he still believes he is indestructible and is prone to showing off. Johnny is in love with Roxanne Simpson, but her father, Quentin Simpson, disapproves of their relationship. Refusing to be separated, the young lovers plan to run off together, but all this changes when Johnny discovers that his father is dying of cancer.

ENTER MEPHISTOPHELES
Mephistopheles is a formidable adversary. A slippery devil with a silver tongue, he interferes in human affairs through his Ghost Riders, and he wants Johnny Blaze to inherit this mantle.

BARTON DIES
Cured of cancer, but not understanding why, an exuberant Barton misjudges a stunt and dies in Johnny's arms.

Before he dies, Barton Blaze gives his beloved Harley Davison, Grace, to his son.

DEVIL'S BARGAIN

Mephistopheles's strength is his ability to exploit the vulnerability of others. Recognizing John Blaze's problems—his desire to be with Roxanne and his father's illness—Mephistopheles offers to cure Barton's cancer in exchange for Johnny's soul. Nicking the young Johnny Blaze's finger with a paper cut, Mephistopheles takes a drop of his blood as agreement. A decision has been made that will change the young man's life forever.

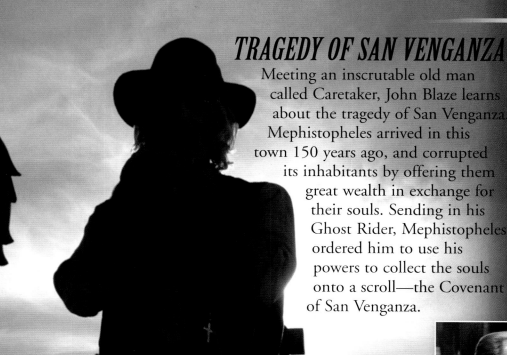

TRAGEDY OF SAN VENGANZA

Meeting an inscrutable old man called Caretaker, John Blaze learns about the tragedy of San Venganza. Mephistopheles arrived in this town 150 years ago, and corrupted its inhabitants by offering them great wealth in exchange for their souls. Sending in his Ghost Rider, Mephistopheles ordered him to use his powers to collect the souls onto a scroll—the Covenant of San Venganza.

SON OF MEPHISTOPHELES
The Caretaker never returned the Covenant to his master, and since then it has become legendary. Mephistopheles's son, Blackheart, is determined to find it, and use it to overthrow his father.

Mephistopheles makes good

Fifteen years on from his original bargain with Johnny Blaze, Mephistopheles returns to make good on their agreement. Although Johnny accuses him of treachery, Mephistopheles refuses to let Johnny back out on his commitment. As the sun starts to set, Johnny begins his first transformation into the demon biker, the Ghost Rider.

BATTLING
BLACKHEART
Transformed into Ghost Rider, Johnny is swept into a series of confrontations with Blackheart and his demonic allies. Although no one else is hurt, the collateral damage is significant.

Choices

Mephistopheles orders Johnny to return Blackheart to him alive. However, Mephistopheles has underestimated this Ghost Rider—unlike his previous servants, Johnny had sold his soul for love. As Blackheart consumes the souls on the Covenant, Ghost Rider uses his Penance Stare to make him revisit his sins. Although he is is returned to his father alive, Blackheart has lost his mind.

ALLIES AND ENEMIES

IN HIS YEARS ON THE ROAD working as a stunt rider for his father or running his own stunt show, Johnny Blaze had met a lot of colorful characters. But none of these compare with the people and creatures he encounters following his first transformation into Ghost Rider. From Mephistopheles to Blackheart, from Caretaker to the Hidden, Johnny would go head-to-head with some of the most powerful creatures in the cosmos.

TORTURED SOUL
Despite his professional success, Johnny is not happy, and only ever finds peace when performing dangerous stunts.

The Hellcycle
After his father's death, Johnny let Barton's beloved motorcycle, Grace, fall into disrepair. However, following Mephistopheles's return, the bike is mysteriously restored to its former glory. During Johnny's first transformation into Ghost Rider, the bike is similarly altered—charged with flame it becomes the Hellcycle.

CARETAKER
After his first night as Ghost Rider, an exhausted Johnny Blaze collapses at the feet of Caretaker. Enigmatic, straight-talking, and wise, Caretaker outlines the history of the Ghost Rider to his young friend. As Johnny's battle with Blackheart escalates, he comes to realize that Caretaker is in fact Carter Slade, his predecessor as Ghost Rider.

JOHNNY'S PLACE
Johnny is so focussed on his stunt career that his garage becomes his home.

Roxanne
Even as a teenager, Roxanne Simpson loved Johnny Blaze. When he turns his back on her after his father's death, she is devastated. Throwing herself into her career she becomes a high-profile TV reporter, only meeting Johnny again many years later.

THE HIDDEN

Blackheart carefully plans how to get the Covenant of San Venganza. Knowing that his father will send a Ghost Rider, he forges an alliance with three elemental demons, Abigor, Wallow, and Gressil. These demons have the ability to hide inside any object, but their power is nothing compared to Blackheart's. Although they distrust him, they fear him even more, and so agree to join him.

ABIGOR   WALLOW   GRESSIL

Elemental demons

Each member of the Hidden possesses a different power. Abigor can control the air, and assault enemies with vicious winds. Wallow uses water as a weapon. Gressil can control fire and attempts to immolate Ghost Rider.

With a stab of his finger, poisonous necroplasm seeps into Blackheart's victims, transforming them into mummified corpses.

Blackheart

Utterly without remorse and greedy for power, the demon Blackheart does not care who dies or how much suffering he causes on his mission to seize the Covenant of San Venganza. He is determined to defeat his father.

1970s

The creation of Ghost Rider resulted from major changes to the comic book industry, which took place in the early 1970s. From 1954 onward, the American comic market had been regulated by the Comics Code Authority (CCA). This introduced stringent guidelines against graphic violence, sexual innuendo, and also horror. However, following a revision of the rules in 1971, horror comics finally made a welcome return to the marketplace. Prior to the establishment of the CCA, Marvel—or Timely as it was called then—had dominated this genre and so it seemed natural for them to explore it once again. In the 1970s, the company's first forays into this area included *Savage Tales*, *Werewolf by Night*, and, of course, *Ghost Rider*. Based on an idea from Gary Friedrich, *Ghost Rider* was first captured on the page by artist Mike Ploog, and championed by editor Roy Thomas. Before long it had become a hit.

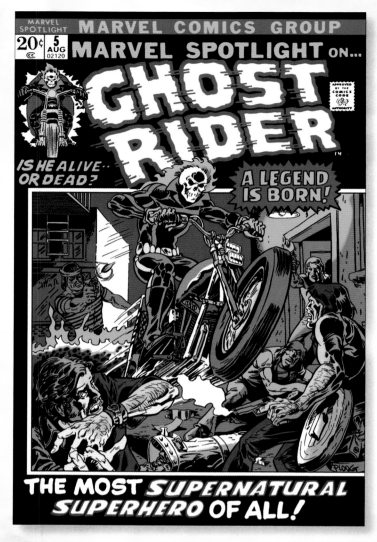

Marvel Spotlight Vol 1, #5 (Aug 1972)
Johnny Blaze makes a bargain with Satan in
Ghost Rider's debut appearance.
(Cover art by Michael Ploog)

1973

Marvel Spotlight *Vol.1 #11 (Aug. 1973)*
Satan's servant, the Witch Woman,
is sent to destroy Johnny Blaze.
(Cover by Rich Buckler and
Mike Esposito)

1973

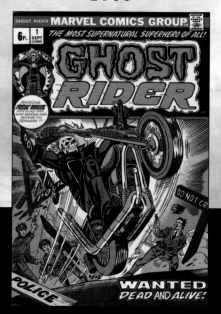

Ghost Rider *Vol. 1 #1 (Sept. 1973)*
Following a successful run in
Marvel Spotlight, Ghost Rider is
given his own comic.
(Cover art by Gil Kane and Jim Mooney)

1975

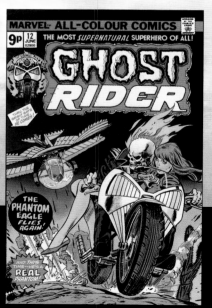

Ghost Rider *Vol. 1 #12 (June 1975)*
Ghost Rider helps the Phantom Eagle
defeat his bête noir—von Reitberger.
(Cover art by Gil Kane, Frank Giacoia
and Klaus Janson)

1975

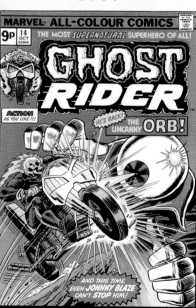

Ghost Rider *Vol. 1 #14 (Oct. 1975)*
After appearing in Marvel Team-Up #15,
the Orb returns in the main series.
(Cover art by Ron Wilson and
Frank Giacoia)

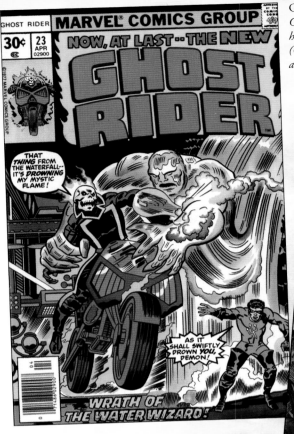

Ghost Rider *Vol. 1 #23 (April 1977)*
Ghost Rider has his first encounter with his wettest adversary—the Water Wizard. (Cover art by Jack Kirby, Joe Sinnott, and Dan Crespi)

Ghost Rider *Vol. 1 #24 (June 1977)*
After two issues shadow boxing the Enforcer, Ghost Rider finally confronts him. (Cover by Gil Kane and Dave Cockrum)

THE CREATORS

Gary Friedrich
After writing various romance and western comics, Gary Friedrich had an acclaimed run on *Sgt. Fury and his Howling Commandos*, earning two Alley Awards for Best War Title. Following *Ghost Rider*, Friedrich worked on other titles, including *Captain America* and *X-Men*, before leaving the industry.

Mike Ploog
Before leaving comics in the mid-70s, Mike Ploog helped launch a number of titles including *Werewolf by Night*, *Ghost Rider*, and *Monster of Frankenstein* (scripted by Gary Friedrich). Recently, Ploog has returned to comics, teaming up with J.M. DeMatteis on *Abadazed* and *Stardust Kid*.

Roy Thomas
By the time he came to edit *Ghost Rider*, Roy Thomas was well-established at Marvel. He has edited countless comics and scripted titles including *Sgt. Fury and his Howling Commandos* and *Conan the Barbarian*. The creator of Red Sonja, Thomas's most recent work is the 2006 one-shot *Red Sonja Monster Island*.

1975

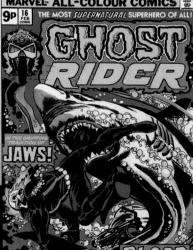

The Champions #1 (Oct. 1975)
Ghost Rider joins the Super Hero team, The Champions... but not for long. (Cover art by Gil Kane and Dan Adkins)

1976

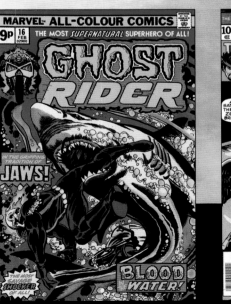

Ghost Rider *Vol. 1 #16 (Feb. 1976)*
Riding the waves created by Steven Spielberg's Jaws*, Ghost Rider battles a shark. (Cover art by Dave Cockrum*

1977

The Champions #10 (April 1977)
The Champions are captured by Darkstar and her fellow Russian agents. (Cover art by Dave Cockrum)

1978

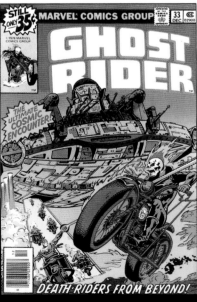

Ghost Rider *Vol. 1 #33 (Dec. 1978)*
One of Ghost Rider's rare encounters with aliens. (Cover art Bob Budiansky and

1970s-1980s

For the early part of its run, the creative team behind *Ghost Rider* was constantly in flux. It was only with issue #26 and the advent of Don Perlin's steady hand on pencils that things began to settle down. "I had just finished a three year stint on *Werewolf by Night*," says Perlin, "and was doing filler work until *Ghost Rider* came along." Perlin was responsible for pencils on some 35 issues of the comic and from issue #36 was joined by writer Michael Fleisher, who stayed in place for a similar 30 issues. A bi-monthly for the first part of its run, with this more stable team and the comic's ongoing success, *Ghost Rider* was made into a monthly comic. When Perlin and then Fleisher eventually left to pursue other projects, J.M. DeMatteis took over writing duties. Despite being praised for his work on *Ghost Rider*, it was during DeMatteis's tenure that the series finally drew to a close.

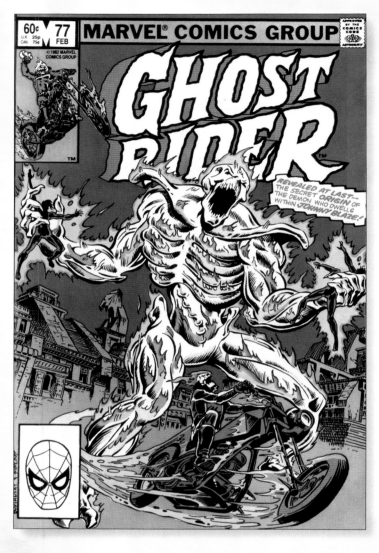

Ghost Rider *Vol. 1 #77 (February 1983)*
At last, after over 80 issues, the origins
of the Ghost Rider are revealed.
(Cover art by Bob Budiansky and Dave Simons)

1979
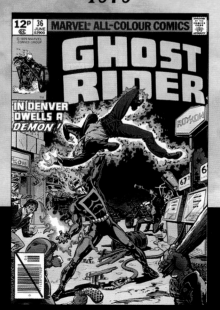

Ghost Rider *Vol. 1 #36 (June 1979)*
Johnny takes a trip to Denver and fights some local barflies.
(Cover art by Bob Budiansky

1980
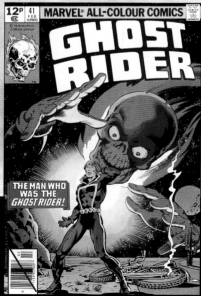

Ghost Rider *Vol. 1 #41 (Feb. 1980)*
After being mugged on a freight train, Johnny loses his memory.
(Cover art by Bob Budiansky

1980
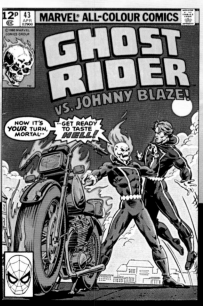

Ghost Rider *Vol. 1 #43 (April 1980)*
Not for the last time, Johnny and Ghost Rider are split apart.
(Cover art by Bob Budiansky

1980

Ghost Rider *Vol. 1 #46 (July 1980)*
Flagg Fargo challenges Johnny for the title of World's Greatest Stunt Rider.
(Cover art by Bob Budiansky

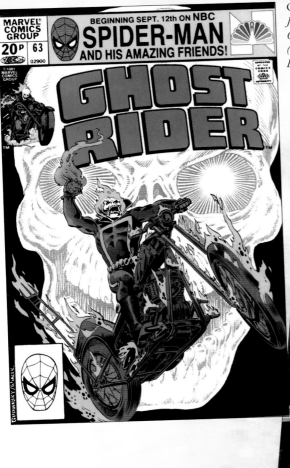

Ghost Rider *Vol. 1 #63 (Dec 1981)*
*Johnny happens across the Quentin
Carnival and becomes its chief stunt rider.
(Cover art by Bob Budiansky and
Bob Wiacek)*

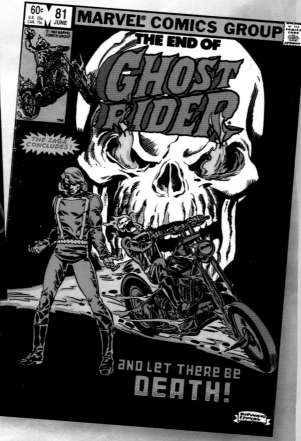

Ghost Rider *Vol. 1 #81 (June 1983)*
*In the final climactic issue, Johnny Blaze gains
his freedom from the Ghost Rider.
(Cover art by Bob Budiansky and Dave Simons)*

THE CREATORS

Don Perlin

A prolific comic book artist, Don Perlin
had been working in the industry for
30 years by the time he came to work on
Ghost Rider. Perlin's work on *Ghost Rider*
followed three years on *Werewolf by Night*,
and preceded a 71-issue stint on *The
Defenders*. Perlin is best known for his
work on Valiant Comics' *Bloodshot*.

Michael Fleisher

Hugely productive for a time, Fleisher
also scripted *Jonah Hex and other Western
Tales*, *Spider-Woman*, and *Conan the
Barbarian*, as well as his 30 issues of
Ghost Rider. Since the mid-80s he has
been largely absent from the comic field.

J.M. DeMatteis

Before his short but notable run on
Ghost Rider, J.M. DeMatteis had worked
on *The Defenders* and *Captain America*.
He went on to a five-year stint on DC's
Justice League International, before
moving on to *The Amazing Spider-Man*.
His most recent work is the fantasy *The
Stardust Kid*, on which he teamed up with
fellow *Ghost Rider* veteran Mike Ploog.

1980

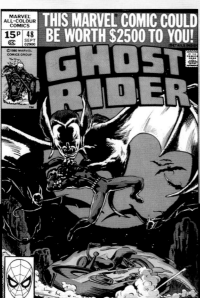

Ghost Rider *Vol. 1 #48 (Sept. 1980)*
*Ghost Rider goes head-to-head with
a colony of vampire bats.
(Cover art by Bob Budiansky and
Bob McLeod)*

1981

Ghost Rider *Vol. 1 #57 (June 1981)*
*More tragedy befalls Johnny Blaze
as he battles Shocks Marley.
(Cover art by Bob Budiansky
and Allen Milgrom)*

1981

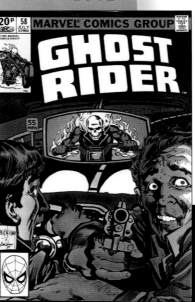

Ghost Rider *Vol. 1 #58 (July 1981)*
*One of the best covers in Ghost Rider
history—it makes you look twice.
(Cover art by Bill Sienkiewicz
and Alan Weiss)*

1982

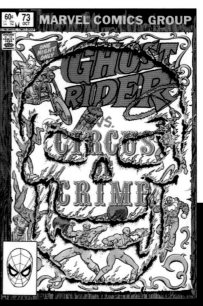

Ghost Rider *Vol. 1 #73 (Oct. 1982)*
*A billboard-style cover, publicizing Ghost
Rider's battle with the Circus of Crime.
(Cover art by Bob Budiansky
and Dave Simons)*

1990s PART 1

When Howard Mackie arrived at Marvel as an assistant editor, one of the first things he asked about was the possibility of bringing back *Ghost Rider*. The year was 1984 and the Brimstone Biker's first run had only ended the year before. Five more years were to pass before editor Mark Gruenwald invited Mackie to write a pitch for the character's return. "I had never written an ongoing series before and I was quite nervous." Mackie says, "Before I went away Mark Gruenwald suggested that I try and base it on a new character and not Johnny Blaze." Although he was not told this at the time, Mackie was just one of several writers invited to pitch, but it was his idea that eventually won the day. Drawing on his own childhood experiences, Mackie's Ghost Rider was to be hosted by one Dan Ketch. Rather than constantly traveling, he would be based in Cypress Hills, Brooklyn, where Mackie himself had grown up.

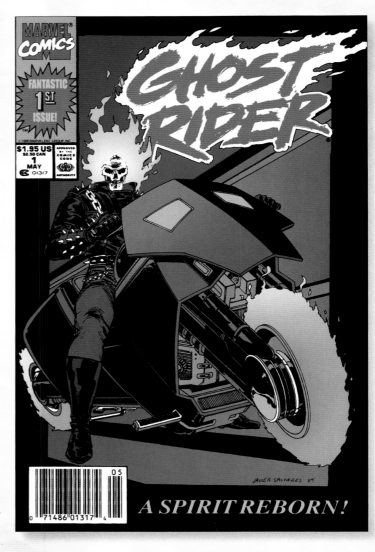

Ghost Rider *Vol. 2 #1 (May 1990)*
After a break of seven years, writer Howard Mackie brings Ghost Rider back.
(Cover art by Javier Saltares)

1991

Ghost Rider *Vol. 2 #11 (March 1991)*
Dan Ketch has his first encounter with Nightmare.
(Cover art by Larry Stroman and Mark Texeira)

1991

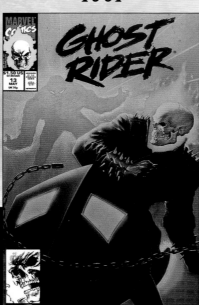

Ghost Rider *Vol. 2 #13 (May 1991)*
Dan Ketch meets John Blaze in the climax of this issue.
(Cover art by James Palmiotti and Mark Texeira)

1991

Ghost Rider *Vol. 2 #15 (July 1991)*
A glow-in-the-dark Ghost Rider—such covers were all the rage in the '90s.
(Cover art by Mark Texeira)

1991

Ghost Rider *Vol. 2 #18 (Oct. 1991)*
Ghost Rider saves Mrs Ketch from the vile Church of Styge.
(Cover art by Nelson DeCastro)

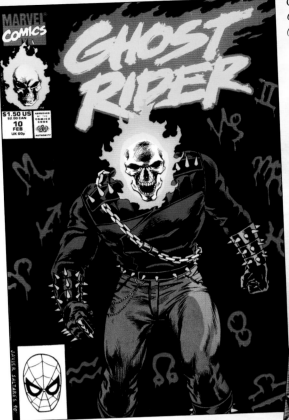

Ghost Rider *Vol. 2 #10 (Feb. 1991)*
Ghost Rider goes up against the psychotic Zodiak.
(Cover art by Javier Saltares)

Ghost Rider *Vol. 2 #14 (June 1991)*
It's showdown time between Ghost Rider
and John Blaze.
(Cover art by Mark Texeira)

THE CREATORS

Howard Mackie

After joining Marvel in 1984, Howard Mackie's work on *Ghost Rider* represented his first stab at writing an ongoing series. As well as contributing to more than 100 issues featuring ol' Flamehead, Mackie has worked on several *Spider-Man* titles and some 35 issues of *X-Factor*. Howard Mackie is currently writing children's books.

Javier Saltares

Artist Javier Saltares bookended *Ghost Rider* Volume 2, performing pencil duties on the first and last issues of this title. His other work includes *David's Mighty Men*—which he created, wrote, and drew—and *Wolverine: Origins & Endings.*

Max Texeira

A regular artistic partner of Javier Saltares, Mark Texeira worked with him on *Ghost Rider* Volume 2's opening and closing issues. He reunited with Saltares on the fifth volume of *Ghost Rider*, which launched in 2006. Texeira is also the creator of the comic *Pscythe.*

1992

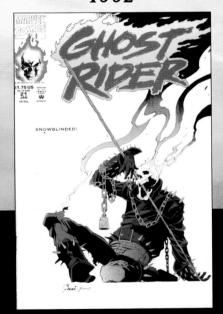

Ghost Rider *Vol. 2 #21 (Jan. 1992)*
A beautifully clean cover pencilled by Joe Quesada.
(Cover art by Joe Quesada and James Palmiotti)

1992

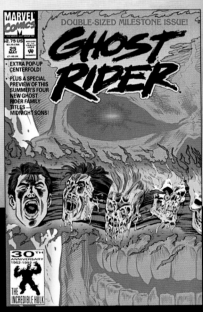

Ghost Rider *Vol. 2 #25 (May 1992)*
This double-length issue also included a pop-up center spread.
(Cover art by Ron Wagner and Mike Witherby)

1992

Ghost Rider *Vol. 2 #28 (Aug. 1992)*
Various Midnight Sons crossover stories were to plague Ghost Rider for 18 issues.
(Cover art by Andy Kubert and Joe Kubert)

1992

Spirits of Vengeance *#1 (Aug. 1992)*
The first spin-off title to capitalize on Ghost Rider's surging popularity.
(Cover art by Adam Kubert)

1990s PART 2

In order to realize Howard Mackie's take on a new Ghost Rider, Marvel editor-in-chief, Tom DeFalco, had to overrule the sales department, who claimed the comic would not sell. To begin with, *Ghost Rider* remained under the radar because it was expected to fail, and Mackie was given a free reign. As a consequence, the first 25 issues are arguably the strongest. "I wanted to do short stories—one or two issues long," said Mackie, "like with Stan Lee's work on *The Amazing Spider-Man*, I wanted the first dozen or so issues to sum up everything *Ghost Rider* was about." Those first 25 issues saw Ghost Rider's first encounters with Blackout, Snowblind, and Scarecrow, and the return of Centurious— characters who would remain in the series for most of its run. Soon sales went through the roof and the doubters were proved wrong. But this success had big implications for the comic. As *Ghost Rider* began to get noticed, Howard Mackie's creative freedom became restricted.

Ghost Rider *Vol. 2 #31 (Nov. 1992)*
Many of these Midnight Sons *comics came
pre-bagged and included a poster.
(Cover art by Andy Kubert and Joe Kubert)*

1992

Spirits of Vengeance #3 (Oct. 1992)
*Ghost Rider and John Blaze battle
Skinner, one of writer Howard Mackie's
favorite creations.
(Cover art by Adam Kubert)*

1992

Ghost Rider *Vol. 2 #30 (Oct. 1992)*
*Nightmare was one of the few villains to
return from* Ghost Rider Volume 1.
*(Cover art by Andy Kubert and
Joe Kubert)*

1993

Ghost Rider *Vol. 2 #34 (Feb. 1993)*
*Death Ninja's debut. (Howard Mackie is
still embarrassed at this character's name!)
(Cover art by Bret Blevins and
Al Williamson)*

1993

Ghost Rider *Vol. 2 #38 (June 1993)*
*The Scarecrow was to become a recurring
nemesis for the Ghost Rider.
(Cover art by Mike Manley)*

118

Ghost Rider *Vol. 2 #32 (Dec. 1992)*
Danny Ketch is brought back to life, and not for the last time, either.
(Cover art by Bret Blevins)

The Original Ghost Rider *#7 (Jan. 1993)*
Original Ghost Rider *reprinted the first 20* Ghost Rider *stories.*
(Cover art by Jeff Johnson and Dan Panosian)

THE CREATORS

Bret Blevins

Artist Bret Blevins worked on *Ghost Rider* Volume 2 from issues 32 through 37. Blevins has contributed to a wide range of comic titles, including *The Incredible Hulk*, *Star Wars*, and *The Dark Crystal*. More recently he has worked on a number of animated television series, including *Superman*, *Batman*, and *Batman Beyond*.

Ron Garney

After entering the comic industry in 1989, Ron Garney provided pencils on *Ghost Rider* Volume 2 for 10 issues, starting with #39. Although he has worked on DC's *Justice League of America* and *Animal Man*, Garney is best known for his contributions to Marvel's *Captain America* and *Silver Surfer*.

Adam Kubert

Adam Kubert was responsible for pencils on the first 13 issues of spin-off title, *Spirits of Vengeance*. He went on to win plaudits for his long run on *Wolverine*, which led to him working as penciller on the launch books for *Ultimate X-Men* and *Ultimate Fantastic Four*.

1993

Ghost Rider *Vol. 2 #43 (Nov. 1993)*
The Missing Link crossover attempted to explain who the Spirits of Vengeance were.
(Cover art by Ron Garney and

1993

Blaze: Legacy of Blood *#1 (Dec. 1993)*
For the first time since 1983, a series was devoted exclusively to John Blaze.
(Cover art by Ron Wagner and Bill

1994

Ghost Rider *Vol. 2 #45 (Jan .1994)*
Part 10 in the 17-issue Siege of Darkness crossover story.
(Cover art by Ron Garney and

1994

Ghost Rider *Vol. 2 #46 (Feb. 1994)*
Following Dan Ketch's death, Vengeance takes over as Ghost Rider.
(Cover art by Ron Garney and

1990s PART 3

Even given the comic boom that was taking place during the early 1990s, *Ghost Rider* sold exceptionally well. Before long the lead character was guesting all over the place, from the *X-Men*, to *Daredevil*, and *Punisher*. Whenever old Ghostie appeared on a cover, sales rose, and so the character quickly became all-pervading. At that time Marvel was grouping many of its ongoing series under umbrella titles. So successful was *Ghost Rider*, it was seen as a good vehicle to launch a new swathe of supernatural series under the *Midnight Sons* banner. *Darkhold*, *Nightstalkers*, *Morbius: The Living Vampire*, and *Ghost Rider*'s own spin-off series, *Spirits of Vengeance*, all resulted from this strategy. For two years Ghost Rider was to feature in a number of intricate stories that crossed between all these titles. Writer Howard Mackie comments, "I always wanted Ghost Rider to be the only supernatural character in the series but as his popularity grew, this became more difficult."

Ghost Rider *Vol. 2 #33 (Jan. 1993)*
In between battling Madcap, Danny is told that he's adopted.
(Cover art by Bret Blevins and Al Williamson)

1994

Spirits of Vengeance #21 *(April 1994)*
The last issues of Spirits of Vengeance focused almost exclusively on John Blaze.
(Cover art by Henry Martinez and

1994

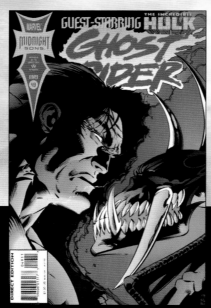

Ghost Rider *Vol. 2 #49 (May 1994)*
Vengeance meets the Hulk, who shares some insights on split personalities.
(Cover art by Ron Garney and

1994

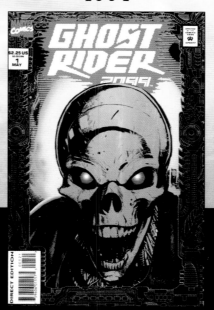

Ghost Rider 2099 #1 *(May 1994)*
A cyberpunk Ghost Rider is created for the Marvel 2099 imprint.
(Cover art by Chris Bachal and

1994

Ghost Rider *Vol. 2 #50 (June 1994)*
This double-length 50th issue boasted a die-cut, foil stamped cover.
(Cover art by Ron Garney and

Ghost Rider *Vol. 2 #61 (May 1995)*
"Alas poor Ghost Rider"—
Stacy Dolan betrays her childhood sweetheart.
(Cover art by Salvador Larroca and Sergio Melia)

Ghost Rider *Vol. 2 #47 (March 1994)*
The demons that curse the Badilino
family continue to wreck havoc.
(Cover art by Ron Garney and
Christopher Ivy)

THE CREATORS

Salvador Larroca
Salvador Larroca was the longest serving artist on *Ghost Rider* Volume 2, working as penciller from issues #51 to #81. Following his time on *Ghost Rider*, Larroca teamed with Chris Claremont for two long stints—on *Fantastic Four* and *X-Treme X-Men*—before joining Warren Ellis on *newuniversal*.

Len Kaminski
The writer on *Ghost Rider 2099*, Kaminski stayed with this title for the whole of its 25-issue run. Kaminski was also responsible for creating the Marvel Super Hero Slapstick and served as scribe on *Bloodshot* Volume 2, from Acclaim Comics.

Chris Bachalo
Providing art breakdowns on the first few issues of *Ghost Rider 2099*, Chris Bachalo helped to define the gritty "in-your-face" style of this cyberpunk title. Bachalo has since brought his idiosyncratic style to bear on *Generation X*, *Uncanny X-Men*, and the Cliffhanger title, *Steampunk*.

1994

Ghost Rider 2099 #3 *(July 1994)*
Based in a cyberpunk dystopian future,
Ghost Rider 2099 even has a flying bike.
(Cover art by Mark Buckingham)

1994

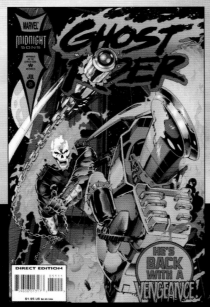

Ghost Rider *Vol. 2 #51 (July 1994)*
No one stays dead for long in comics.
Within four issues of his death, Ghost
Rider was back.
(Cover art by Salvador Larroca)

1994

Ghost Rider *Vol. 2 #52 (Aug. 1994)*
A new potential ally for Ghost Rider,
Shriker arrives on the scene.
(Cover art by Ron Garney)

1994

Blaze #1 *(Aug. 1994)*
Ghost Rider's success led to a fourth
spin-off title focusing on John Blaze.
(Cover art by Henry Martinez and
Bud Larosa)

1990s PART 4

As with issue #69, *Ghost Rider* writer Howard Mackie decided it was time to step back from ol' Flamehead, and Ivan Velez took up scripting duties. Velez's objectives were simple: "I wanted to flesh out Ghost Rider's backstory, but I also wanted to explore Dan Ketch's character some more." Under Velez's stewardship, the stories became longer and more intricate and he began to detail the character's origins. Unfortunately, the comic boom was now over and changes to the comic's artwork were proving unpopular—vibrant inks and a Manga artistic style did not sit well with Ghost Rider's brooding character. With sales in steep decline, Velez was forced to wrap things up in issue #93 although he still had some exciting plans for Ghost Rider: "I wanted Dan to live on without the Ghost Rider," Velez explains, "and around issue #100 I was going to have Johnny volunteering to become a new Ghost Rider, but hosting Noble Kale, not Zarathos." Sadly it wasn't to be.

Ghost Rider *Vol. 2 #87 (Aug. 1997)*
Writer Ivan Velez begins his final Ghost Rider story arc.
(Cover art by Pop Mhan)

1995

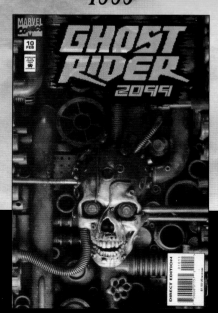

Ghost Rider 2099 #10 (Feb. 1995)
A rare photographic cover, similar in style to Taggart's work on Doom Patrol.
(Cover art by Tom Taggart)

1995

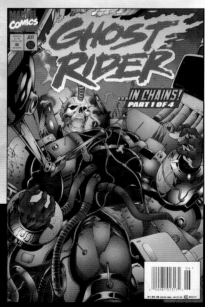

Ghost Rider *Vol. 2 #62 (June 1995)*
Ghost Rider is imprisoned in Containment Facility #24601.
(Cover art by Salvador Larroca and Sergio Melia)

1995

Blaze #12 (July 1995)
In this final issue of Blaze, *John Blaze was reunited with his children.*
(Cover art by Gary Erskine)

1995

Ghost Rider *Vol. 2 #68 (Dec. 1995)*
The X-Men, Gambit and Wolverine unite with Ghost Rider against the alien Brood.
(Cover art by Salvador Larroca and Sergio Melia)

Ghost Rider *Vol. 2 #93 (Feb. 1993)*
Volume 2 draws to a close.
(Cover art by Javier Saltares and
Mark Texeira)

Ghost Rider *Vol. 2 #92 (Jan. 1998)*
Dan Ketch finally frees himself
of the Ghost Rider curse.
(Cover art by Javier Saltares and Mark Texeira)

THE CREATORS

Ivan Velez
Ivan Velez served his comic book apprenticeship with Milestone Comics, for whom he wrote the award-winning *Blood Syndicate* and *Static.* His two years on *Ghost Rider* were one of his first forays into mainstream comics. He is perhaps best known for *Tales of the Closet,* a graphic novel about eight gay teenagers living in Queens.

Larry Hama
Acclaimed for his work on the comic book *G.I. Joe,* Larry Hama was responsible for writing the twelve issues of *Blaze,* another *Ghost Rider* spin-off title. As well as scripting titles that included *Generation X* and *Wolverine,* Hama was the creator of *Bucky O'Hare* for Continuity Comics.

Ron Wagner
Responsible for pencils on several issues of *Ghost Rider Volume 2,* Ron Wagner went on to perform similar duties on *Blaze: Legacy of Blood.* Elsewhere in comics, Wagner has undertaken art chores on *Batman, G.I. Joe,* and *Punisher.*

1996

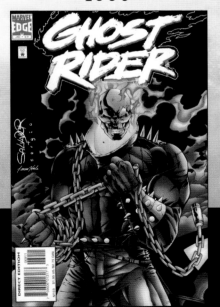

1996

1996

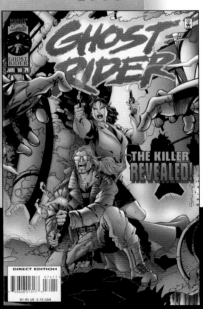

1997

Ghost Rider *Vol. 2 #69 (Jan. 1996)*
After scripting more than 100 Ghost Rider comics, Howard Mackie puts down his pen
(Cover art by Salvador Larroca, Sergio

Ghost Rider 2099 *#22 (Feb. 1996)*
A stand-out cover from the brilliant Ashley Wood.
(Cover art by Ashley Wood)

Ghost Rider *Vol. 2 #74 (June 1996)*
Vengeance is exposed as a serial murderer.
(Cover art by Salvador Larroca and Sergio Melia)

Ghost Rider *Vol. 2 #82 (Feb. 1997)*
Manga and Howard the Duck meet Ghost Rider—the omens for 'ol Flamehead weren't good.

2000s

Following Ghost Rider's demise in 1998, the character has returned twice. Devin Grayson's 2001 miniseries, *The Hammer Lane*, neatly sidestepped much of Ghost Rider's more complicated back story. Instead, it served as a homage to the essence of the original character. With a Ghost Rider movie on the horizon, fan favorite Garth Ennis was invited to give his take on the character in 2005. In his own words, Ennis "didn't know much" about Ghost Rider and so felt able to introduce a certain freshness, such as providing a more heaven-versus-hell take on Ghost Rider's supernatural origins. From Ennis's point of view, "Those elements give you the most impressive visuals. There's a nice apocalyptic feel you get when you're filling the skies with hosts of warrior angels." The success of Ennis's six-issue mini series—*Road to Damnation*—guaranteed the launch of a new ongoing series. Written by Daniel Way, this new *Ghost Rider* title kicked off in July 2006.

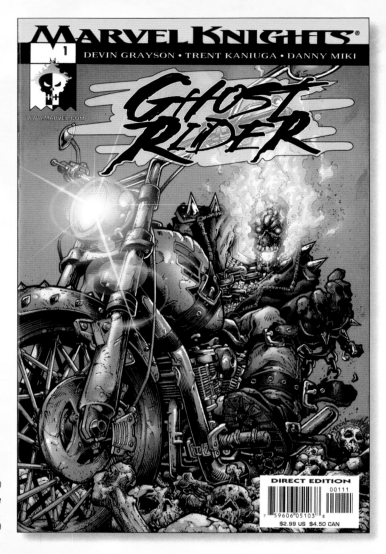

The Hammer Lane #1 (Aug. 2001)
Ghost Rider returns and this time it's John Blaze's turn to bear the brimstone biker.
(Cover art by Trent Kaniuga, Danny Miki, and Dan Kemp)

2001

Ghost Rider: The Hammer Lane #3
(Oct. 2001)
Gunmetal Gray hunts down Ghost Rider.
(Cover art by Trent Kaniuga, Danny

2001

Ghost Rider: The Hammer Lane #4
(Nov. 2001)
Ghost Rider strikes back.
(Cover art by Trent Kaniuga, Danny

2002

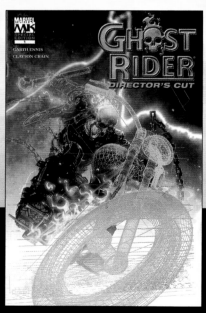

Ghost Rider: The Hammer Lane #6
(Jan. 2002)
John Blaze heads back on the road.
(Cover art by Trent Kaniuga, Danny

2005

Ghost Rider: Road to Damnation #1
(Sept. 2005)
This "Special Edition" included the original pitch and script.

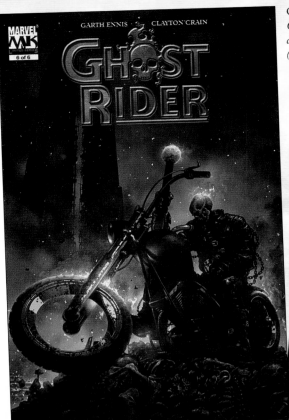

Ghost Rider: Road to Damnation #6 (Feb. 2006)
Garth Ennis's short run as Ghost Rider scribe concludes in classic Ennis style.
(Cover art by Clayton Crain)

Ghost Rider: The Hammer Lane
#1/2 (July 2001)
Limited edition exclusive to Wizard magazine readers
(Cover art by Trent Kaniuga, Danny Miki, and Dan Kemp)

THE CREATORS

Devin Grayson

Writer Devin Grayson's script for *The Hammer Lane* was followed by work on various mainstream titles, including two years on *Batman: Gotham Knights* and a five-year run on *Nightwing*, which ended in 2005. Returning to Marvel, she assumed writing chores on *X-Men: Evolution*.

Garth Ennis

Acclaimed writer Garth Ennis is probably best known for his work on the much-praised *Preacher*, co-created with Steve Dillon. Ennis first broke into American comics with his three-year run on *Hellblazer* and he has since attached his name to a range of titles including *The Punisher*, *The Authority*, and *303*.

Clayton Crain

Before his work on *Road to Damnation*, Clayton Crain had also worked on Marvel's *Venom vs. Carnage* mini-series. Other credits for Crain include *Curse of the Spawn* and *KISS: Psyche Circus*.

2005   **2005**   **2005**   **2006**

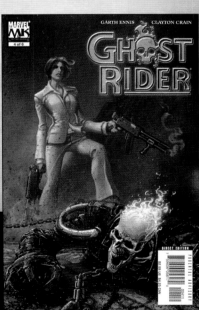
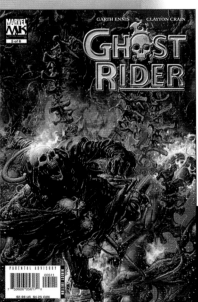

Ghost Rider: Road to Damnation #2
(Oct. 2005)
Road to Damnation opens with John Blaze in hell.

Ghost Rider: Road to Damnation #4
(Dec. 2005)
On the hunt for the demon Kazann, Ghost Rider battles the Archangel Ruth.

Ghost Rider: Road to Damnation #5
(Dec. 2005)
Kazann is let loose on Texas. Cripes!
(Cover art by Clayton Crain)

Ghost Rider *Vol. 5 #1 (July 2006)*
Daniel Way picks up Ghost Rider where Garth Ennis left him—in hell.
(Cover art by Clayton Crain)

INDEX

Abigor 109
Alhazared, Jimmy 105
aliens 64, 113, 122
America, Captain 76
Angel 34
Atlantis 78, 80
Ayers, Dick 6
Azmodeus 37, 41

Baal 99
Bachalo, Chris 121
Badilino, Michael 63, 69, 74–5,
    79, 90–92
Badilino family 12, 68, 74, 88,
    121
Blackheart 13, 17, 65, 94–7,
    107–8
Blackout 52, 62, 64, 70, 71,
    72–3, 78, 118
Black Rose 95–7
Black Widow 34–5
Blade 81
Blaze 119, 121, 122, 123
Blaze, Barton 12, 22, 27, 56,
    106, 109
Blaze, Craig 13, 86, 88–9, 99
Blaze, Dan 12, 13
Blaze, Emma 13, 86, 88–9, 99
Blaze, Johnny 7, 13, 17,
    20–47, 79, 84
    beomes Ghost Rider 24–5,
        100–101
    and The Champions 34–5
    at Copperhead Canyon 32–3
    and Dan Ketch 50, 53, 66–7,
        80–81, 116
    enemies of 38–41, 44–6
    family of 13, 86, 88–90,
        98, 99
    in hell 13, 102–3
    motorcycle of 29, 30–31
    in movie 106–9
    powers of 28–9, 58
    and Quentin Carnival 42–3,
        86–7, 98
    romances 36–7, 42
    and Roxanne 13, 23–5, 27,
        36, 47, 86–7
Blaze, Naomi 12, 13, 17, 52,
    53, 56–7, 97

Blaze, Roxanne 46, 108
    as Black Rose 95, 97
    childhood 22
    death of 67, 90, 99
    family of 13, 86–9
    kidnapped 33, 38, 89
    love for Blaze 23–5, 27, 36,
        47, 106
Blevins, Bret 119
Blevins, Holden 98
Blood 10, 12, 14, 15, 67, 68,
    69, 74, 80, 88
Brood 64, 122
Buchanan, Sam 80, 81
Buttview 102

Caretaker 15, 50, 65, 67–9,
    75, 88, 107–8
Centurious 13, 44–5, 69, 71,
    75, 118
    bargain with Mephisto 17, 44
    and Dan Ketch 50, 58
    and the Firm 45, 73
    and Johnny Blaze 47, 86–7
    kidnaps Francis Ketch 62
    and Lilith 79
Champions 34–5, 113
Chicago 37
Choam 91
Christ's Crown 65, 94–5
Circus of Crime 43, 115
Clara 86
Claremont, Chris 121
Clarke, Stuart 35
Clothilde 43
Cochrane, Harrison 104
Cochrane, Kenshiro "Zero" 104
Code: Blue 65, 92
comics 112–25
Comics Code 6, 7, 112
Copperhead Canyon 32–3
Covenant of San Venganza 107, 109
Crain, Clayton 125
Creed 78
Crimson Dynamo 34
Crumm, Lucy 94–5
Cult of Zarathos 44
cybernetic warriors 104–5
Cypress Hills Cemetery 50,
    56, 57, 59, 70

D/Monix 104
Daniels, Chris 75
Daredevil 36, 64
Daredevil comic 6, 120
Darkhold 80, 120
Darkstar 25, 113
D'Auria, Jack 65
Death Ninja 71, 118
Death's-Head 35
Deathwatch 57, 70–73, 91
Debbie 37
Deep Throat 63, 91
DeFalco, Tom 118
Delazny Studios 36
DeMatteis, J.M. 113, 114, 115
Denver 37
Doghead 96
Dolan, Capt. Arthur Gerard 63
Dolan, Stacy 53, 60–61, 63,
    76, 92, 121
Drake, Frank 81
Dread 91
Dwarf 81

Eliot the Clown 43
Ellis, Warren 129
Empire State Building 73
Enforcer 39, 113
Ennis, Garth 124, 125

Fallen 80, 81
Fargo, Flagg 40, 114
Firm 45, 73, 76, 79
flame bike 30–31
Fleisher, Michael 114, 115
Fowler, Red 43
Freakmaster 43
Friedrich, Gary 6–7, 112, 113
Furies 12, 16, 54, 55, 93, 95
Fury, Nick 92

Gambit 122
Garey, Ron 119
George 89
Ghost Rider 6–7, 112–25
Ghost Rider 2099 104–5, 120, 121
Ghost Rider: the Movie 106–9,
    124
"Ghost Riders in the Sky" 6
Ghost-Works 104, 105

Goodman, Martin 6
Gray, Gunmetal 101, 124
Grayson, Devin 124, 125
Great Vincenzo 43
Greenland, Northern 78
Gressil 109
Grimley, Gloria 37
Gruenwald, Mark 116
Gustav, Earl 102

Hag 71
Hama, Larry 123
Hammer Lane, The 124
Hand 64
Harrison, Norman 77
Hastings, Prof. Louise 80, 81
hell 13, 102–3, 125
Hellfire Chain 50, 58
Hellgate, Anton 67, 75, 90–91
Hellstrom, Daimon 33, 36
Hercules 34, 35
Hidden 88, 89, 109
Hobgoblin 65
Holly 46
Hollywood 35, 36
Hoss 102, 103
Hotwire Martyrs 104
Howard the Duck 123
Hulk 120

Icebox Bob 98, 99
Iceman 34–5
International Contractors 70

Kale family 12, 16, 52, 54, 68, 88, 96
Kale, Jennifer 93
Kale, Magdalena 12, 54, 93, 95
Kale, Naomi, see Blaze, N.
Kale, Noble 12, 13, 16, 54–6,
    93, 95, 96–7
Kale, Pastor 54–5
Kaminski, Len 121
Kazann 102–3, 125
Ketch, Barbara 12, 13, 52,
    57, 60, 62, 68, 72
Ketch, Dan 12, 13, 50–53,
    57–81, 93, 95, 97, 122–3
    allies of 64–5, 68–9, 75
    becomes Ghost Rider 52–3,
        57, 62

death and resurrection of 81,
  84, 90, 97, 119
enemies of 70–79
and John Blaze 50, 53, 66–7, 116
and Midnight Sons 80–81, 84
motorcycle of 59
powers of 58–9
and Stacy Dolan 53, 60–61
Ketch, Francis 52, 53, 60, 62, 68,
  116
King, Hannibal 81
Kingpin 70, 71, 72
Kubert, Adam 119
Kylie 105

Langtree, Gina 36
Larroca, Salvador 119
Lee, Stan 6–7
Lilin 78, 80, 81
Lilith 50, 65, 68, 69, 72,
  75, 78–9, 80, 81
Littletree, Linda 33
Loan Shark 43
Loughton, Ebenezer 76

Mackie, Howard 116–18, 120,
  122
Madam Olga 43
Madcap 120
Magazine Enterprises (M.E.) 6
Malachi 13, 102–3
Manga 123
Marianne 89
Marley, Shocks 115
Marvel Comics 6, 112–25
Marvel Spotlight 7
Medallion of Power 12–17,
  54–6, 68, 69, 74, 79, 95
Mephisto 12, 16–17, 65
  and Badilino 69, 74–5
  and Centurious 17, 44
  death of 94–5, 96
  and Johnny Blaze 24–7,
    32–3, 41
  and Kale family 55, 56, 57
  and Zarathos 14–15
Mephistopheles 106–8
Midnight Sons 61, 65, 69,
  79, 80–81, 84
Midnight Sons 117, 118, 120

Milner, Katy 36
Mole 39
Montesi, Victoria 80, 81
Morbius 80, 81, 120
Mount of Meditation 15
movie 106–9, 124
Murdock, Matt 35, 36

New York 50, 64, 70, 77, 90
Next Wave 92
Nightmare 45, 116, 118
Nightstalkers 81, 120
N.Y.P.D. 60, 61, 63, 74, 76, 90
  see also Police Special Task Force

Olympus 35
Orb 27, 38, 112

Page, Karen 35, 36
Pao Fu 96–7
Patience 54–5
Penance Stare 50, 58, 74, 75, 77,
  93, 107
Perlin, Don 114, 115
Phantom Eagle 112
Pilgrim 78
Piston 101
Ploog, Michael 7, 112, 113
Pluto 34, 35
Police Special Task Force 60, 61,
  74, 92
Punisher 65, 94
Punisher comic 120

Quentin, Ralph 42
Quentin Carnival 13, 42–3, 79,
  86–7, 89, 98, 115
Quesada, Joe 117

Rak 91
Rampage 34, 35
Randolph, Cynthia 42
Red Sonja 113
Regent 88–9
Road to Damnation series 102–3,
  124–5
Ruth, Archangel 103, 125

Saltares, Javier 117
Samuels, Curly 26

San Venganza 107
Satan's Servants 26
Sacrecrow 76, 118
Seer 69, 88, 89
Shannon, Drake 38
S.H.I.E.L.D. 61, 92
Shriker 65, 121
Simpson, Crash 13, 17, 22, 24–7,
  38, 42
Simpson, Mona 22–4, 27, 45
Simpson, Roxanne,
  see Blaze, Roxanne
Sin Eater 46
Skinner 78, 118
Slade, Carter 6, 108
Snakedance 32, 33
Snowblind 91, 118
Sokolowski, Lt. "Ski" 61, 92
Soul Crystal 13, 44, 45, 47,
  79, 86
Spider-Man 38, 65
Spirits of Vengeance 12, 14,
  15, 119
  Badilino as 74
  destroyed and recreated 80, 96
  Ghost Rider as 55–8, 101
Spirits of Vengeance 117, 120
Stanton, Sally 37
Strange, Dr. 65, 80, 81, 93
Stunt-Master 35
Stygian Church 45, 62, 79, 116
Succubus 64
Suicide 71, 75, 77
Super Heroes 34, 113
Swarm 34

Tabicantra 37, 41
Texeira, Max 117
Thomas, Roy 112, 113
Troll 71

Uriel 12, 16, 55

Van Zante, Peter 39
Velez, Ivan 122, 123
Vengeance 63, 69, 74–5, 90,
  93, 123
  becomes Ghost Rider 119, 120
Venus 35
Verminus Rex 96

Void 45
Von Reitberger 112

Wagner, Ron 123
Wallow 96, 109
Warbot 104–5
Water Wizard 39, 113
Way, Daniel 124, 125
Wei, Linda 73
Wendigo 99
West Coast Super Heroes 34
Williamson, Ron 37
Witch Woman 112
Wolverine 64, 65, 92, 94, 122
Wood, Ashley 123

X-Men 64, 122
X-Men comics 120

Zarathos 12, 14–15
  battles against 61, 69, 75, 80–81
  and Centurious 44–5, 79
  Ghost Rider as 25, 45, 66
  and Mephisto 16
  reborn 79
Zero 104–5
Zeus 35
Zodiak 35, 75, 77, 117
zombies 91

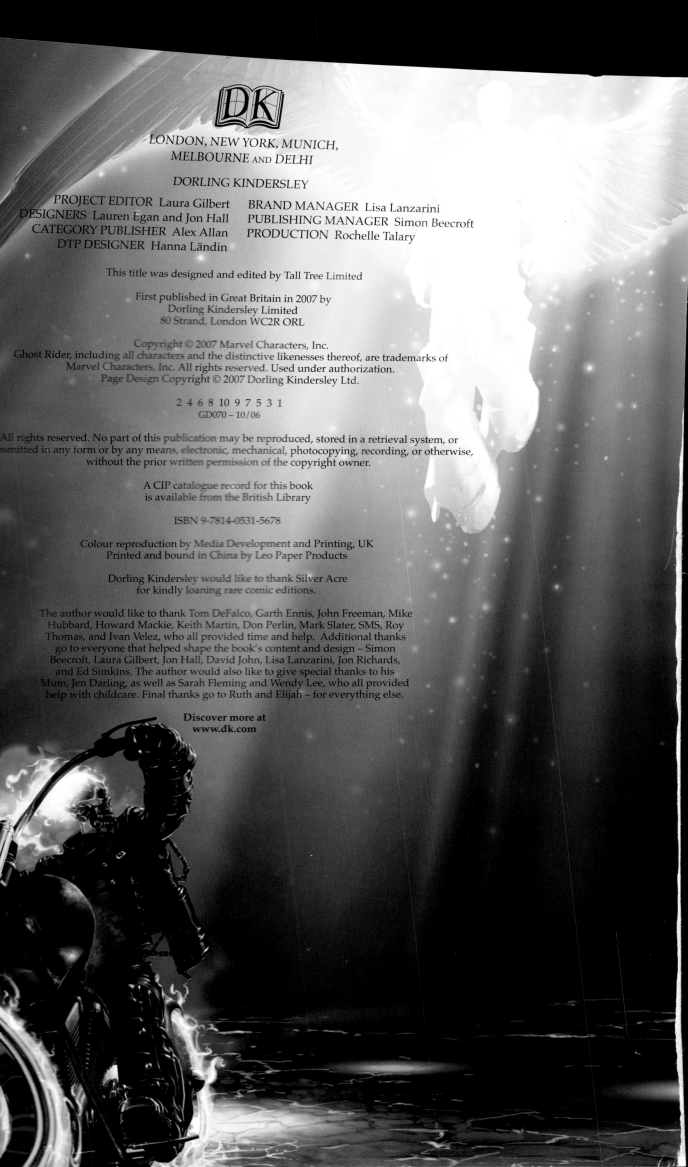

DK

LONDON, NEW YORK, MUNICH,
MELBOURNE AND DELHI

DORLING KINDERSLEY

PROJECT EDITOR Laura Gilbert   BRAND MANAGER Lisa Lanzarini
DESIGNERS Lauren Egan and Jon Hall   PUBLISHING MANAGER Simon Beecroft
CATEGORY PUBLISHER Alex Allan   PRODUCTION Rochelle Talary
DTP DESIGNER Hanna Ländin

This title was designed and edited by Tall Tree Limited

First published in Great Britain in 2007 by
Dorling Kindersley Limited
80 Strand, London WC2R ORL

2 4 6 8 10 9 7 5 3 1
GD070 – 10/06

A CIP catalogue record for this book
is available from the British Library

ISBN 9-7814-0531-5678

Colour reproduction by Media Development and Printing, UK
Printed and bound in China by Leo Paper Products

Dorling Kindersley would like to thank Silver Acre
for kindly loaning rare comic editions.

The author would like to thank Tom DeFalco, Garth Ennis, John Freeman, Mike
Hubbard, Howard Mackie, Keith Martin, Don Perlin, Mark Slater, SMS, Roy
Thomas, and Ivan Velez, who all provided time and help. Additional thanks
go to everyone that helped shape the book's content and design – Simon
Beecroft, Laura Gilbert, Jon Hall, David John, Lisa Lanzarini, Jon Richards,
and Ed Simkins. The author would also like to give special thanks to his
Mum, Jen Darling, as well as Sarah Fleming and Wendy Lee, who all provided
help with childcare. Final thanks go to Ruth and Elijah – for everything else.

Discover more at
www.dk.com

death and resurrection of 81, 84, 90, 97, 119
enemies of 70–79
and John Blaze 50, 53, 66–7, 116
and Midnight Sons 80–81, 84
motorcycle of 59
powers of 58–9
and Stacy Dolan 53, 60–61
Ketch, Francis 52, 53, 60, 62, 68, 116
King, Hannibal 81
Kingpin 70, 71, 72
Kubert, Adam 119
Kylie 105

Langtree, Gina 36
Larroca, Salvador 119
Lee, Stan 6–7
Lilin 78, 80, 81
Lilith 50, 65, 68, 69, 72, 75, 78–9, 80, 81
Littletree, Linda 33
Loan Shark 43
Loughton, Ebenezer 76

Mackie, Howard 116–18, 120, 122
Madam Olga 43
Madcap 120
Magazine Enterprises (M.E.) 6
Malachi 13, 102–3
Manga 123
Marianne 89
Marley, Shocks 115
Marvel Comics 6, 112–25
Marvel Spotlight 7
Medallion of Power 12–17, 54–6, 68, 69, 74, 79, 95
Mephisto 12, 16–17, 65
and Badilino 69, 74–5
and Centurious 17, 44
death of 94–5, 96
and Johnny Blaze 24–7, 32–3, 41
and Kale family 55, 56, 57
and Zarathos 14–15
Mephistopheles 106–8
Midnight Sons 61, 65, 69, 79, 80–81, 84
Midnight Sons 117, 118, 120

Milner, Katy 36
Mole 39
Montesi, Victoria 80, 81
Morbius 80, 81, 120
Mount of Meditation 15
movie 106–9, 124
Murdock, Matt 35, 36

New York 50, 64, 70, 77, 90
Next Wave 92
Nightmare 45, 116, 118
Nightstalkers 81, 120
N.Y.P.D. 60, 61, 63, 74, 76, 90
see also Police Special Task Force

Olympus 35
Orb 27, 38, 112

Page, Karen 35, 36
Pao Fu 96–7
Patience 54–5
Penance Stare 50, 58, 74, 75, 77, 93, 107
Perlin, Don 114, 115
Phantom Eagle 112
Pilgrim 78
Piston 101
Ploog, Michael 7, 112, 113
Pluto 34, 35
Police Special Task Force 60, 61, 74, 92
Punisher 65, 94
Punisher comic 120

Quentin, Ralph 42
Quentin Carnival 13, 42–3, 79, 86–7, 89, 98, 115
Quesada, Joe 117

Rak 91
Rampage 34, 35
Randolph, Cynthia 42
Red Sonja 113
Regent 88–9
Road to Damnation series 102–3, 124–5
Ruth, Archangel 103, 125

Saltares, Javier 117
Samuels, Curly 26

San Venganza 107
Satan's Servants 26
Sacrecrow 76, 118
Seer 69, 88, 89
Shannon, Drake 38
S.H.I.E.L.D. 61, 92
Shriker 65, 121
Simpson, Crash 13, 17, 22, 24–7, 38, 42
Simpson, Mona 22–4, 27, 45
Simpson, Roxanne,
   see Blaze, Roxanne
Sin Eater 46
Skinner 78, 118
Slade, Carter 6, 108
Snakedance 32, 33
Snowblind 91, 118
Sokolowski, Lt. "Ski" 61, 92
Soul Crystal 13, 44, 45, 47, 79, 86
Spider-Man 38, 65
Spirits of Vengeance 12, 14, 15, 119
   Badilino as 74
   destroyed and recreated 80, 96
   Ghost Rider as 55–8, 101
Spirits of Vengeance 117, 120
Stanton, Sally 37
Strange, Dr. 65, 80, 81, 93
Stunt-Master 35
Stygian Church 45, 62, 79, 116
Succubus 64
Suicide 71, 75, 77
Super Heroes 34, 113
Swarm 34

Tabicantra 37, 41
Texeira, Max 117
Thomas, Roy 112, 113
Troll 71

Uriel 12, 16, 55

Van Zante, Peter 39
Velez, Ivan 122, 123
Vengeance 63, 69, 74–5, 90, 93, 123
   becomes Ghost Rider 119, 120
Venus 35
Verminus Rex 96

Void 45
Von Reitberger 112

Wagner, Ron 123
Wallow 96, 109
Warbot 104–5
Water Wizard 39, 113
Way, Daniel 124, 125
Wei, Linda 73
Wendigo 99
West Coast Super Heroes 34
Williamson, Ron 37
Witch Woman 112
Wolverine 64, 65, 92, 94, 122
Wood, Ashley 123

X-Men 64, 122
X-Men comics 120

Zarathos 12, 14–15
   battles against 61, 69, 75, 80–81
   and Centurious 44–5, 79
   Ghost Rider as 25, 45, 66
   and Mephisto 16
   reborn 79
Zero 104–5
Zeus 35
Zodiak 35, 75, 77, 117
zombies 91

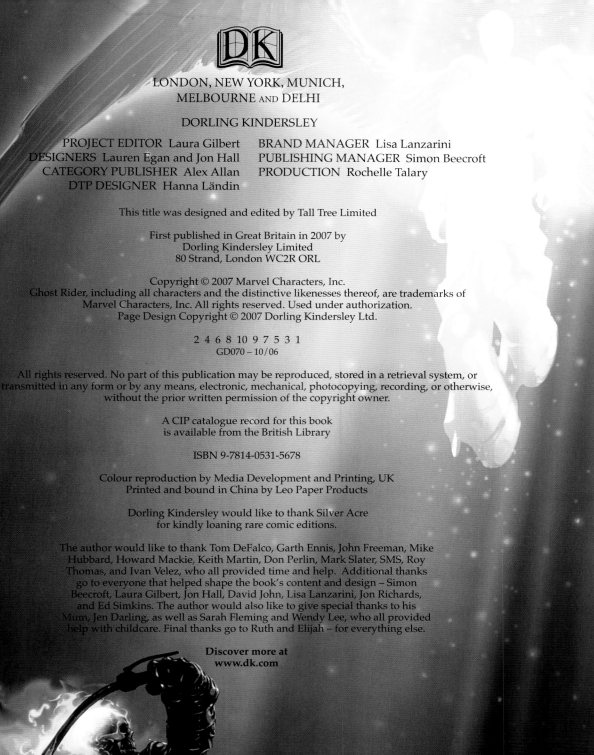

DK

LONDON, NEW YORK, MUNICH,
MELBOURNE AND DELHI

DORLING KINDERSLEY

PROJECT EDITOR Laura Gilbert   BRAND MANAGER Lisa Lanzarini
DESIGNERS Lauren Egan and Jon Hall   PUBLISHING MANAGER Simon Beecroft
CATEGORY PUBLISHER Alex Allan   PRODUCTION Rochelle Talary
DTP DESIGNER Hanna Ländin

This title was designed and edited by Tall Tree Limited

First published in Great Britain in 2007 by
Dorling Kindersley Limited
80 Strand, London WC2R ORL

2 4 6 8 10 9 7 5 3 1
GD070 – 10/06

A CIP catalogue record for this book
is available from the British Library

ISBN 9-7814-0531-5678

Colour reproduction by Media Development and Printing, UK
Printed and bound in China by Leo Paper Products

Dorling Kindersley would like to thank Silver Acre
for kindly loaning rare comic editions.

The author would like to thank Tom DeFalco, Garth Ennis, John Freeman, Mike
Hubbard, Howard Mackie, Keith Martin, Don Perlin, Mark Slater, SMS, Roy
Thomas, and Ivan Velez, who all provided time and help. Additional thanks
go to everyone that helped shape the book's content and design – Simon
Beecroft, Laura Gilbert, Jon Hall, David John, Lisa Lanzarini, Jon Richards,
and Ed Simkins. The author would also like to give special thanks to his
Mum, Jen Darling, as well as Sarah Fleming and Wendy Lee, who all provided
help with childcare. Final thanks go to Ruth and Elijah – for everything else.

**Discover more at
www.dk.com**